Praise for *Treasures in Dark P¹*

"Dr. Leanna Cinquanta is a spiritual d⌐
not be more excited about what Gr   ⌐d
the Gospel and rescue the broken i.   ere are
few more qualified than Leanna to wr⌐   ⌐ading fear-
lessly into the forgotten and dark plac⌐   ⌐th to reveal the
light and hope of Jesus and pull out the ⌐   ⌐n those trapped in a
hopeless existence.

"*Treasures in Dark Places* is compelling, heart-wrenching and beautifully written. Leanna reminds us that the need in the earth may be
great, but our God is so much greater. By reading Leanna's call into
ministry, her commissioning into the harvest field and ultimately her
inspiring impact and transformative work in the nation of India, your
faith will be awakened that you, too, are able to pierce darkness in
the face of human tragedy—as 1 John 5:4 assures us, 'Everyone born
of God overcomes the world.'"

Dr. Ché Ahn, founding pastor, HROCK Church, Pasadena,
California; president, Harvest International Ministry;
international chancellor, Wagner Leadership Institute

"Do you ever get tired of mundane, lifeless 'Churchianity' and long
for the God of the Bible to burst out of man-made boxes and into
action? If so, wait no longer. Leanna Cinquanta has experienced the
compassion and power of God at work today and has captured some
of those stunning stories in her book. Your heart will burn and your
faith will be activated as she takes you on her journey of mystery and
revelation, trial and triumph."

James W. Goll, founder, God Encounters; bestselling
author; international speaker; Life Languages trainer

"I remember Leanna as a wide-eyed 23-year-old who came to YWAM
Denver eager to find her place in God's Kingdom. From the very start
she displayed a wholehearted passion to help others. I never imagined,
however, that she would end up doing a fraction of the amazing things
she has. Her life is a testament to this fact: God will use anyone whose
life is completely surrendered to Him. *Treasures in Dark Places* is the
powerful account of a young woman willing to leave the comfort

and security of a promising career to serve God wherever He would lead—and He led her to one of the most difficult places on earth. You won't be able to put this book down until you've read the very last page. It is engaging and inspiring, but what is most astounding is that the stories you're about to read are all true."

Peter Warren, director, Youth With A Mission Denver

"A remarkably crafted tool for the laborer seeking to plant churches among the unreached. This is an unforgettable hands-on account of a highly motivated pioneer opening new territory. Leanna learned to hear the voice of God, understood His heart for a desperate people group and assembled a team of local workers to get the job done. They became an 'emergency response team' that released victims trapped by the enemy's earthquake, healed their wounds and set them on the pathway to the clearing in which God's love is the total source of light. A gripping story!"

Ken Urban, frontier missions advocate,
Youth With A Mission Denver

"In this masterfully painted account of sacrifice and triumph, your fears will be dispelled and your faith rocketed to new heights. Called to one of the darkest parts of the world—known as the 'graveyard of Christianity'—Leanna Cinquanta went to northern India alone, not knowing if she would ever return. Not only did she thrive, but Leanna raised up key indigenous leaders, catalyzing a massive movement that leads tens of thousands of people to Christ every year. Today Leanna's team oversees 23,000 home-based churches, 160 children's education centers, several schools and an aggressive ministry to eradicate human trafficking in the most dangerous part of the world. *Treasures in Dark Places* delivers a jolt of Holy Spirit power, vision and purpose. Leanna will take you into her world where 'impossible' does not exist and where a God of miracles enables even the least likely person to change the world."

Wesley Campbell, director, Be a Hero

"Rarely does a literary work juxtapose poignant narrative and powerful mission in such a balanced manner. This book is a must-read for anyone with God's heart for the most vulnerable in the most difficult places. Leanna weaves her tome masterfully in a manner that will leave the reader changed forever."

Barry Christopher Howard, CFO and senior vice president of
finance, human resources and administration, World Relief

"For a decade I have known and worked with Leanna and many of the dear believers we both count as treasures. This is book-of-Acts territory and proof that the Gospel is the greatest force on earth. I commend to you her adventure and pray you will share in it."

Dr. Tom Hatley, pastor, Immanuel Baptist Church
Global Outreach Center, Northwest Arkansas

"Leanna is a practitioner, not just a theorist. When I met her in India, she went by the title Sis, but she was raising up indigenous leaders to empower the people and rescue children. The Lord has given her eyes to see what others don't see yet—treasures in everyone!"

Dr. Mark D. Tubbs, U.S.A. director, Harvest International Ministry

"Brilliant. Simply brilliant! This extraordinary, true story of how God has used the life of a woman totally surrendered to Him to help change a nation inspires and challenges us all to make our lives count for the Kingdom."

Felicity Dale, author, *An Army of Ordinary People* and
The Black Swan Effect; coauthor, *Small Is Big*

"I met Leanna and heard her story for the first time in 1999. The anointing of the Holy Spirit was so strong when she was talking that all I could do was weep. Leanna is walking in the calling of God, and *Treasures in Dark Places* will release a newness and a higher purpose into your life. May all who read this pray for and support her world-changing initiatives."

David Ford, CEO, SMI Services, Jamestown, North Carolina

"Kudos for your writing and for your amazing ministry in India. It's a privilege to work with you and help get your message out. You have a fabulous gift for storytelling. This book is absolutely riveting!"

Christy Philippe, freelance writer and editor,
HarperCollins, TimeWarner, Thomas Nelson,
Baker Books, Chosen Books and Random House

Praise for Leanna Cinquanta and TellAsia's work in India

"Leanna is the most competent field missiologist I have ever known."

Dr. C. Peter Wagner (1930–2016), vice president, Global Spheres Inc.; founding chancellor, Wagner Leadership Institute

"No agency I'm aware of has a greater heart, a better organization or a more comprehensive plan to reach the tough areas of the world."

Dr. Tom Hatley, former chairman, International Mission Board; senior pastor, Immanuel Baptist Church, Rogers, Arkansas

"She speaks a bold clarion call to step aside from small ambitions into an inheritance of impacting the world."

from *The Black Swan Effect*

"Nuclear."

Mike Constantz, director of missions, Saddleback Church, Lake Forest, California

"Leanna has an anointing that far exceeds that for local churches, but which is for cities and regions."

Dick and Arleen Westerhof, European Economic Summit, Amsterdam

"Leanna Cinquanta is a pure antidote to complacency. She leaves hearts that are burning with the zeal of the Lord and motivated to do their part in the transformation of nations, starting right where they are. She is global impact wrapped in a tiny frame and releases both personal heart challenge and world-changing strategies."

Charles and Ann Stock, Life Center Ministries, Harrisburg, Pennsylvania

Treasures
IN DARK PLACES

Treasures
IN DARK PLACES

One Woman, a Supernatural God
and a Mission to the Toughest Part of India

LEANNA
CINQUANTA

Chosen

a division of Baker Publishing Group
Minneapolis, Minnesota

Published by Chosen Books
11400 Hampshire Avenue South
Bloomington, Minnesota 55438
www.chosenbooks.com

Chosen Books is a division of
Baker Publishing Group, Grand Rapids, Michigan

Printed in the United States of America

Library of Congress Cataloging-in-Publication Data
Names: Cinquanta, Leanna, author.
Title: Treasures in dark places : one woman, a supernatural god and a mission to the toughest part of India / Leanna Cinquanta ; foreword by Gary Wilkerson.
Description: Minneapolis, Minnesota : Chosen, a division of Baker Publishing Group, [2017]
Identifiers: LCCN 2016034854 | ISBN 9780800798161 (trade paper : alk. paper)
Subjects: LCSH: Cinquanta, Leanna. | Missionaries—India—Biography. | Church work with children—India.
Classification: LCC BV3269.C44 A3 2017 | DDC 266.0092 [B] —dc23
LC record available at https://lccn.loc.gov/2016034854

Cover design by Rob Williams, InsideOutCreativeArts

Contents

Foreword

*E*very so often God raises up a work so astounding it begins to impact a nation. Church history is filled with examples of men and women of God whom He has used to lead such endeavors.

In the last century we saw the launch of great ministries such as the Billy Graham Evangelistic Association, Campus Crusade for Christ, World Vision and a work my own father started called Teen Challenge. These all began at nearly the same time and were deeply blessed and internationally impactful.

In our generation God is once again doing such a work through Leanna and the TellAsia Ministries team. I have been graced to see with my own eyes this wonderful work of God. In northern India, one of the most hardened, unreached and difficult areas of the world, Leanna is pioneering and leading a work that is transforming a nation. Christ is being exalted, and thousands of churches have been planted. Miracles of healing and salvation occur daily and come in waves.

I've been around ministry and missions a long time. I have heard many grand visions that had no real evidence of resulting in change nor were they led by those with the capacity to see such a vision unfold. It might be tempting to think the same concerning Leanna and TellAsia Ministries. When this young woman set off alone for north India, many expected her to be just another missionary casualty. But instead, the unique approach God showed her resulted in astounding results. God proved that He has indeed "chosen the weak things of this world to confound the things which are mighty" (1 Corinthians 1:27 KJV).

Today, TellAsia's vision to end child trafficking and illiteracy among millions of needy children may seem overzealous. I, like Doubting Thomas, would not have believed it unless I had touched this work personally. But God is doing it! Leanna's team through TellAsia Ministries is well on their way to seeing this vision become a reality. The Lord is empowering these humble believers to press on to complete their formidable goal. Much work is still to be done, but it is clear that the Holy Spirit is the source behind the successes.

Treasures in Dark Places will stir your faith, capture your heart and renew your vision to believe for the impossible. But most of all it will bring glory to God, and that is why this book was written. It's all about the love, goodness and power of God . . . and how He works through unpretentious, single-minded vessels who only want His glory to be known.

I thank God for Leanna, and I thank God that she wrote this book. Read it at your own risk. Your heart will be stirred, and there's no telling what God might call forth in your own life.

Gary Wilkerson

Prologue

Starlit Eyes

Regret not your attempt at laying siege to
    darkness,
matter not the endeavor's apparent futility.
You may only be a small light passing
    through,
but groping multitudes now seeing the way,
will reach the dawn.

The wadded scar tissue of a butchered amputation trembled. With her remaining hand she thrust a steel bowl toward me, shaking a few coins in the bottom. Though less than twelve years of age, her face no longer expressed the softness of a child nor even the femininity of a girl. Blackened by an amalgamation of sunburned pigment and street grime streaked with rivulets of sweat, her cheekbones gave way to bloodshot eyes sunk deep in her skull. Beggar by day and sex slave by night, she had been debased to a robot existing for the lewd pleasure of her torturers. Hardened by pain and abuse, not a shred of hope remained in her once-lovely face. The spark of life had drained from her eyes, now cold black pits devoid of life. Physically and emotionally she had been twisted and maimed, made into a beast, spirit broken, will and feelings decimated. Hers was a cold existence bereft of love, stripped of dignity, entombed while yet living.

"Jyoti!"

A voice made its way to my ears through the din of horns and bus engines and hawkers shouting their wares. Emerging from my entrancement, I remembered where I was. The bus stand. With my Indian friends. Setting out for a remote village.

Across the crowded street Vincent's lanky frame filled the bus entrance. He motioned with his hand. "Hurry! Bus is leaving."

The engine gunned—the driver's "all aboard" signal.

The girl remained rooted, staring at me, bowl extended. Like the desperate fingers of a drowning wretch, her eyes reached to the core of my being, fastened themselves there and held me. To pull away would rip my heart in two. My soul was engulfed in the horror that composed her life. What could I do? How could I rescue her? I couldn't. I was helpless.

The bus horn blasted—"last call."

"Sister Jyoti, come NOW!"

My hand made an impulsive dive into my backpack's front pouch but stopped short. The brothel owner would relieve her of the day's coin collection the moment she returned for night duty. Instead I yanked a banana from the bunch procured moments earlier from a hawker. At least she could eat a banana. With regretful reverence I placed my offering in her bowl, then tore myself away. Legs propelled my body to the bus, but my soul had been taken captive, utterly disturbed and forever, irreparably infected with the vision of this human tragedy.

The Roadways bus jolted and banged along a narrow strip of broken blacktop, its battered steel frame held together with half-stripped bolts. Swerving or screeching to an abrupt slowdown every few seconds it narrowly avoided a continuous stream of hazards including cyclists, pedestrians, goats, carts pulled by oxen, and crevasses in the pavement sufficient to snap an axle. My native friends had insisted that I occupy the prime spot on the bench we had managed to secure—the window seat. Even so, four of us were crammed into a space made for two and a half. Our fourth team member's leftmost pelvic bone clung precariously to the last inch of seat, his knees enduring the pushing and shoving of those packed in the aisle like upright sardines. The twenty-pound video projector, too precious to risk leaving with the rest of our gear up front in the bus cockpit, occupied both my lap and Janardhan's, and by the second hour, it had rendered my legs numb. I gleaned valuable millimeters of extra body room by letting my elbow protrude daring inches beyond the half-open window, but at risk of losing it to a passing vehicle. Here in northern India the game of "chicken" has been perfected and refined to an art form and I had by now given up the white-knuckled-cringe-and-wait-for-the-crash saucer-eyed terror that grips rookies at their first spin on an Indian road.

A diagonal crack bisected the thin slab of glass constituting my window. Loosely fixed in a metal track, it rattled back and forth at every jolt and jounce but managed not to shatter. On the seatback ahead of us ripped upholstery exposed the seat's urethane innards and provided a convenient pocket where other passengers had deposited candy wrappers and empty chewing tobacco packets.

The roar of the ancient diesel Tata died, replaced by the tortured screech of shoeless brakes hitting the drums. The bus rocked to a near standstill, rolled forward and bumped down off a ledge. Then the engine gunned and we lurched forward once more. Pavement behind, dust billowed up on either side of the lumbering steel box, obscuring vision. The monsoon had long passed and not a drop of precipitation had touched this dirt road in weeks. Though passengers dutifully slid their windows shut, the powdery brown haze still boiled in, blanketing us with grime. But hardly a cough or sneeze was heard for men had already fished in their pockets for *rumals* and women had engaged the ends of their *saris*. In moments the brown hands of the hundred-some passengers on the 38-seater bus pressed makeshift dust masks over nose and mouth and continued their ride unflurried.

Krishna leaned across Janardhan and me to peer out the window. Scanning the landmarks, he searched for a clue to our whereabouts. Soon he exclaimed, *"Aa gaya, chalo!"* We had arrived, and there was no time to lose, because exiting the bus is the most difficult part of the ride.

Seated on the aisle, the job of plowing the way fell to Vincent, who enjoyed the advantage of unusual height for an Indian. From my position by the window the task of squeezing even a slender body past the solid mass of humanity clogging the full length of the aisle appeared futile. But in India, whether fitting people or vehicles through an impossibly tight space, another inch can always be found. Nobody says "Excuse me" because such etiquette is superfluous in a world with no room to step aside. When the bodies involved are metal, back-and-forth maneuvering eventually results in the two vehicles managing to scrape past each other. When bodies are flesh, space is created not by maneuvering but by squishing. Shoulders provide a culturally acceptable means of creating inches where none exist. So Vincent pushed himself into the aisle-standers, and the rest of us followed with our noses in one another's backs to preserve those precious inches he created. Janardhan clutched the video projector against his chest. Thus we progressed steadily forward until at last I glimpsed ahead, protruding above the press of black scalps, a welcomed sign—the vertical steel pole marking the exit.

The bus shuddered to a halt and passengers piled out, jostling and shoving and tripping over feet, oblivious to whether the person they pushed was an old lady or a child. Making ourselves as thin as possible against the front partition of the bus to avoid being trampled, Janardhan transferred the video projector to me. Mindful of his near-complete blindness, it had been previously agreed that I would convey the fragile piece of technology down the stairs while he served as rear-guard to prevent me being shoved. Meanwhile Krishna and Vincent hoisted the rest of our gear onto their shoulders and we piled out into welcomed fresh air and elbow room.

Teenaged Krishna's bright eyes assessed the luggage and the man- and woman-power present, then swiftly began dividing the goods into four piles. These villages were his home, and the worn sandals precariously held to his calloused feet by a single toe loop knew the rocky paths. We stood at the edge of the northern plains where fertile fields and spreading Banyans gave way to rocks and plateaus and dust. *Naxalite* gangsters ruled this territory, and terrorized poverty-stricken villagers and the police folded to bribes partly out of convenience and partly to prevent their wives becoming widows.

17

No buses or rickshaws traveled between here and Krishna's village, so foot power would have to suffice.

"Saman zyada hai, bhaya," muttered a puzzled Krishna, who couldn't decide how we would transport one particularly cumbersome element of our gear, the sixty-pound generator. After a good deal of discussion a decision was reached. Vincent and Janardhan would trade off lugging the generator and a backpack bulging with rolled-up sheet, rope, stabilizer and extension wires while Krishna and I managed with the rest, which included, besides the projector, a two-foot speaker box, amplifier and mic and a jug of kerosene. So off we trooped lining out behind our guide, dust poofing rhythmically from beneath sandals. Squinting into the scorching afternoon sun, sweat cascaded down our faces and its gritty salty rivulets found their way into our mouths. The *dupatta* scarf, an essential element of feminine attire in rural India, added unwelcomed layers of insulation across my shoulders, and my neck itched desperately beneath its sweat-soaked polyester. Rocks in the path occasioned whoever trod immediately ahead of Janardhan to call out, *"Dekho JD, patr!"* JD bent his face downward, straining to see the hazard ahead. Though slowing and stepping carefully, he still usually stumbled on the rock. Even so he hummed a tune, his undefeatable optimism brightening the air.

The rest of us joined in, our spirits rising in celebration of the One who had freed us from bondage, who had loved us unto death and triumphed to give us life . . . the One whose love and salvation a new village would receive tonight for the first time since the world began.

After an hour or so the frequency with which Vincent and JD traded off carrying the generator attested to their growing fatigue, and my shoulders ached from the weight of the projector, encased in the mountaineering backpack

Mom had ingeniously redesigned to fit it. Our path skirted a bluff and crossed a field then disappeared into a shady grove. Wherever there is a bunch of trees on the Indian plain, there is also a village.

The narrow path wound between mud huts stuccoed with the image of an occasional god or goddess, the lone color amidst browns. Bony cows with bulging bellies lazily chewed their cud. Ponderous buffaloes, black hairless hides twitching to repulse the occasional fly, eyed us from their three-foot tethers. Goats with ever-mischievous motley-colored faces and tiny mouths and nimble feet darted here and there, searching for morsels that nobody else considered edible.

Ladies squatting in the doorways of their huts sifted tiny pebbles out of the evening meal's rice or pulverized spices between two stones. Skinny-armed toddlers with wide, hungry eyes and bloated bellies watched us from beneath thatched eaves. Their parents hoped the black string around their waists and heavy mascara smeared around their eyes would fend off the demons. Two boys of about five ventured out as we passed. They wore buttonless shirts that may have once been a color. Man-sized belts wrapped twice around suspended pants with broken zippers. They tagged along behind us, brown faces full of timid curiosity.

Men hovered in the shadows, weathered and hardened from relentless labor. Their dark eyes stalked us from beneath heavy brows emanating a mistrustful chill. Were JD able to see their faces, he might have maintained a degree more reserve in his greeting. Instead he grinned and waved and called out in the local dialect, "Bring family and friends to village square at seven o'clock. You receive ocean of mercy!"

The children gained confidence and more joined the troop. Shouting and jostling they trotted behind appealing for further details. We heightened their curiosity with a provocative "Come and see!"

I thought any moment we'd arrive at Krishna's home, but my optimism dwindled when he marched on with hardly a sideways glance and no offer to explain. My mastery of Hindi still insufficient to afford much conversation, the discipline of "wait and see" proved more practical and less embarrassing. So I stewed in my questions as out the other side of the village we tramped.

Our tail of children halted at the village edge as if having met an unseen boundary. For a few moments they stood gazing after us then cavorted back to their huts. On we trudged, leaving the village behind.

Before us stretched a deserted wasteland, barren of grass and treeless apart from an occasional shrub, littered with garbage. The ground was not sandy but packed mud adobe-hard and scarred with gorges cut by water. This was not a desert but a flood plain. Ahead materialized green cattails and beyond them, sparkling in the final afternoon rays of sunlight, flowed a great river. Still there wasn't a sign of civilization. The unasked questions buzzing in my brain increased. What business did we have in the community dump? Why had we left behind the people for whom we'd come?

"*Jaiiii Masih kiiiii!*" A voice strong and jubilant boomed across the plain. A man approached whose persona struck me as that of Moses descending Mount Sinai. His face shone with a radiance from deep within, and his smile injected me with a thrilling rush of the proximity of heaven. He strode toward Vincent, who responded with another "*Jay Masih ki!*"—"Victory to Christ!"—the Christian adaptation of the traditional Hindu greeting "Victory to Ram."

The men embraced with hearty thumps on the back. "Moses" acknowledged Krishna with a fatherly squeeze before turning to the oddball—me.

"*Saroj Bhaya,*" announced Vincent. "This is Sister Jyoti. Sister Jyoti, meet Brother Saroj." Not long into my foray to India the natives had bestowed upon me the name *Jyoti,* which means "Light." "You brought light into our darkness," they said. "We were alone in our vision to reach our homeland here in the north. Missionaries came and did their best, but they didn't pay much attention to us. They put their own faces out front. But you believe in us, the native people. You realize the time has come for us to reach our own people. He has used you to bring His light into the darkness of our land. Together we will rescue the people from oppression and slavery."

And so here I was. But at this point having arrived only a few months ago, my role was unclear. For the time being, the natives perceived the video projector I'd brought over to be the greatest piece of technology since the wheel, and the videos I'd acquired in the big city now fueled journeys to new villages, in which I felt privileged to participate. My primary contribution involved handling the video projector. Having operated no gadget more sophisticated than a bicycle, the sleek black piece of futuristic technology intimidated them. So I enjoyed my little niche as the tech-savvy American lady with the cool equipment by which a whole village could imbibe the message of God's love and salvation.

"*Chalo, ghar!*" Saroj beamingly summoned us to follow him to his house. Vincent made a fatigued move to pick up the generator but Saroj beat him to it. Hoisting it to his shoulder, he running-walked ahead of us, excited to introduce us to his family. "Give me that!" Vincent tugged on my projector pack. Relieved of his own burden, he would have none of a female bearing more than himself, but I hesitated. Whoever awaited at Saroj's house might now perceive me as the burden-less, pampered, wimpy foreigner. Vincent persisted so I reluctantly relinquished the pack.

Traversing the riverbank I scanned the terrain in search of the house that I now understood to be our destination. But all that appeared were cattails and water-hewn mud ditches and rocks and the occasional rodent scurrying for cover. Krishna had disappeared but now reemerged on a rusted-out cycle that creaked with every depression of the pedals. Onto it they loaded the generator and Krishna walked the cycle while Saroj balanced the load.

Ahead, camouflaged against the brown and green, almost concealed behind a rise, stood a chicken coop. Barely five feet at its peak, the walls were roughly woven from the reeds bobbing along the river's edge. Supported by tree branches for rafters, the same reeds composed the roof. Old clothes and plastic bags served as shingles, held down by bits of rubbish collected from the nearby garbage dump. When afforded freedom the cackling fowl make good use of daylight hours to range far and wide scratching for edibles so the absence of chickens was easily explained. *Odd, though,* I thought, *that a chicken coop would have nothing but a rag for a door. The foxes and weasels around here must enjoy fine dining.* Too small to house a cow, I reconsidered the possibility of its use as a goat shed.

Sweaty grime had collected between my toes and I imagined the pleasure of sitting down and dipping my feet in some cool water. I strained my eyes on ahead, intent on glimpsing the house. *We must be getting close since we've come to where they keep their animals,* I thought. *Maybe their house is a riverfront.* My mind wandered. There it was. A smooth wooden dock. I gratefully unbuckled my sandals and plunged headfirst into cool waters. Then I crawled out, wrapped myself in a towel and lay back in an armchair while imbibing an icy Coke.

"Hallooooo!" Saroj bellowed a greeting.

I snapped back to reality. My comrades ahead had drawn up in front of the chicken coop. Before I could fish my senses out of the imaginary armchair, from the rag-covered doorway of what I had supposed to be an animal shelter emerged a woman and two scruffy children clutching her dress.

Saroj either ignored my gaping mouth and incredulous expression or, I hoped, hadn't noticed. He proudly introduced us to his wife, Rita, from whose wizened face shone the same overcoming joy. Though teeny and frail in appearance, when she grabbed me in a grandmotherly bear hug, her bony arms possessed unexpected strength. Eyes gleaming with emotion, she touched her cheek to mine first on the right then the left, the traditional gesture by which traditional Indian women say, "I'm very pleased to meet you!"

Saroj was urging his daughter to greet me. Half letting go of her mother's *sari*, the six-year-old inched forward. "Tell your name," Saroj prompted. Dirty face and tattered skirt could not shroud the cherubic loveliness of this burnished angel. Eyes darting self-consciously from her mother to me, she murmured in Hindi, "My name is Priya." Then with a giggle she dove behind her mother and peeked out with one eye.

Her little brother, gaining courage, presented himself and stuck out a hand. "My name is Arjun."

I shook his hand. "*Jai Masih ki,* Arjun!"

Amidst the greetings I kept looking about, certain there must be more to this home. Surely if I looked hard enough I'd spot metal trunks containing clothes, a cabinet with dishes and pots and a form of transportation besides that old cycle. But I was wrong. This family owned no more than two sets of clothes each. The only pot simmered on the cow dung fire flickering in a hearth molded of mud on the ground outside the hut. Apart from a meager bag of rice, the only sign of food was a bitter gourd termed *karela* having the appearance of a hybrid warty toad and green frog.

This is the definition of poverty, I thought.

Then I knew I was wrong. This was not the definition of poverty. Poverty is a middle-class family that has no joy. Poverty is a wealthy family enslaved to fear and strife. According to the economy of the world, Saroj and Rita were poor. They lacked education. They lacked financial opportunity. They lacked what the developed world considers necessities of life.

But absence of material possessions hadn't dampened Saroj and Rita's joy. They were no longer slaves. They had escaped the chains under which their kinsmen labored. They had found Jesus, and with Him they had found peace and purpose. Now they walked with the authority of the King of whose kingdom they had become citizens. They were wealthy with a wealth no money could buy. The strangest notion swept over me. I stood in the presence of true royalty.

Transformation begins with the spiritual, with aligning ourselves to God's plan and purpose. Because these children's parents had received Christ, the doorway to God's blessing now lay open, and beyond death lay an eternity of joy. But as I gazed at the children, such knowledge afforded disturbingly scant solace from the deep-down uneasiness and turmoil in my soul. Questions writhed about in my brain. *What future do these children have? Will they reproduce their parents' material deprivation? Will they, in the wake of countless other underprivileged rural Indian children, be abducted and brutalized into sex slavery, or compelled to labor twelve hours a day in a factory?*

From a safe distance Priya and Arjun gazed wide-eyed and wondering at the oddity that was me. A homo sapien wearing light-colored skin hadn't wandered into their secluded habitat since the days of the British *raj*. But today being stared at like a zoo animal didn't trouble me. At least these children were gaining exposure to a brand-new mind-expanding truth: "The world is bigger than our village."

Out of the little shack Saroj carried the only furniture—two cots. Their wobbly legs supported wooden frames with rough hemp laced across hammock-like. In the absence of chairs we perched gratefully on the wooden rail, taking care neither to slip backward onto the sagging string nor to sit in the middle of the long side lest it break.

Upon a guest's arrival to an Indian home the standard and promptly undertaken act of hospitality is to serve up a steaming cup of sweet milky *chai* tea. Those without access to milk still serve that which they have. So from a bucket by the hut Priya dipped water with a steel cup, pouring it into four more cups balanced on a platter. Adding a bowl of coarse sugar and a spoon, she served us. When I took my cup and the proffered spoonful of sugar poured into my palm, Saroj glanced askance at Vincent and queried, "She foreigner . . . no drinking our water! She get sick!"

Having already drained his cup Vincent laid back on the string cot and stretched. "Jyoti isn't a foreigner. She eats and drinks our food and water. She's entirely Indian!"

I confirmed his statement with a confident smile and ventured a bit of Hindi. "Yep, my stomach's become Indian!" Saroj raised his eyebrows with a mixture of amazement and respect as I thrust out my cup for a refill of the brown-tinted fluid.

Though my stomach had learned to cope with the rigors of Indian bacteria, my intestines were still trying to catch up and I was at the moment plagued with serious gastric discomfort. But I hadn't come to India for a luxury cruise. Such trivia did not merit my complaining.

In India, rural families live in close-knit groups. Law and order is minimal, and being separated from the group puts one at great risk from vandals and gangs. So when the chit-chat around the little hut turned to why the family lived in such a deserted place, my Hindi receptors strained to catch the words.

"Before we find Jesus, every day we live in fear of demons and spirits," said Saroj. "We visit holy place to find God but no happy, no peace in family. When we choose follow Jesus, peace and happy come in our home. We remove idol from our house and stop going to temple. Instead now we read Bible and pray. Now we no more fear. When we tell our neighbors they amazed to hear of God who love us and die for us and rise again from grave. They ask questions about Jesus and how they too can have peace and eternal life. But then witch doctor find out! He tell our neighbors because we remove idol from our home, the gods will curse whole village.

"From then on everyone's attitude change. They start to talk bad things about us and mock us. One day the village elders come in group and stand out front of our house. Rita scared they going to beat us. I scared too but I know Jesus give us courage. I put Rita and kids in back of house and step out to meet them. They say, 'Either bring idol back in your house or leave village immediately.' So, here we are."

Vincent's expression displayed concern. "So do they know we're showing the video tonight? Won't they stop us?"

Saroj chuckled. "They know I invite guests from city to come and show movie. No entertainment out here and rarely a visitor. So they curious to see why you come all this way. I expect they sit and watch our movie. Afterward we see what happen."

The shadows grew long. Time to set up the equipment had arrived. We gathered in a circle to pray. After inviting the Lord's presence this night to bring peace and freedom to more of Saroj and Rita's neighbors, we set out for the village.

Having decided the light-skinned creature was in fact human, and discovering I could even manage a few words of Hindi, Priya and Arjun had overcome their bashfulness. One on my left and one on my right, they gripped and caressed my hands. Shining brighter than the stars, their eyes shamelessly stared into my face.

"Auntie, how long you stay in India?"

"Auntie, what is America like?"

"Auntie, teach me English!" Children in India respectfully address older girls or women as "auntie."

I told them of America but avoided describing our plush houses, smooth roads, glitzy malls, technological wonders or material comforts lest they feel deprived.

While I taught them phrases in English, a cry of sadness rose up in my heart. Behind their eyes so full of life and hope, malnutrition lurked. If my gut was hurting from bacteria, theirs was hurting from cold, hard hunger. Their father's inability to afford a private school was obvious. Standards of education in the rural public schools were dismal. "Outcaste" Dalit children such as these, shunned by those of "higher birth," faced mistreatment and discrimination. Without an education, their lives would be forced to recycle another generation of subsistence-level endurance of a harsh existence that daily challenged their will to live.

For now their tender age and innocence shielded them from such weighty thoughts. Nimble as deer they negotiated gullies and hopped over bushes as we walked. Feet full of hope, hearts full of expectation—optimism that would soon be worn to despair by the stranglehold of a suppressive reality. Ardently trotting beside my rugged leather sport sandals, their dusty feet in broken plastic flip-flops would likely travel no farther than the nearby town.

Their little hands, already roughened from living in a world of dirt and rocks, would have no chance to operate a computer or turn the key of a motorized vehicle. They would exist on lentils and rice, plagued by constant hunger pains and hunted by disease. They would pass their days in a narrow and primitive world, living in mud or thatch shacks and laboring in the field to eke out an existence, chained to poverty by debt and by a cruel system that views suffering as well-deserved penance for sins in a former life.

I longed to give these children three nutritious meals a day, and a good education including their dream of learning English. I longed to set them up for a bright future. And how many more similar to them or in far worse conditions? At least these children had two parents who loved them. Others didn't. Three hundred million people in spiritual and physical slavery. Seventy-five million of them children, and of those thirty million destitute, orphaned or at risk of abuse. Their rescue and freedom was why I had come.

But now that I was here, what was I to do? At least tonight, this village would learn of Jesus' love. A few would turn to Him. Tonight, some would be rescued from the spiritual chains. The point at which deliverance must begin was spiritual transformation. Afterward and along with it would come the physical, educational and economic.

Priya's gaze still searched me and her hand still gripped mine. I squeezed it back but dared not look into her eyes or she would have seen tears in mine. Their faces blended with the face of the maimed beggar girl. The thought of their bleak future threatened to crush my heart. I, too, was once six years old. I was also the daughter of low income parents. But I grew up in America. I had access to education, and was born in a land of reasonable justice where everyone willing to work hard could come up in life. Not so for an Indian child born into the same situation. A girl child whose father had abandoned the family, or whose mother had died, was likely to follow in the footsteps of the wretched girl I had seen hours ago, whose deathlike gaze still tormented my soul.

Throughout my quarter century of life, Mystery had been preparing its charge for this embarking. But now as I walked on under the vast canopy of stars with the children's hands clutching mine as if I embodied the fulfillment of their impossible dreams, I felt altogether impotent and helpless. The light in this rag-clad six-year-old's eyes would only shine for a few more years until the reality of suffering wiped out her hope. How long before I could give her a better future?

1

Mystery in the Night

Mystery waits its chance to bring awe and wonder into life. It trails us, shadowing our movements but glimpsed from the corner of our eye. Mystery sees neither race nor color, popularity nor obscurity, privilege or challenge. It refuses to bow to that which life's unfairnesses have decreed for us. Mystery sees what we can become. It envisions a brighter future and helps us pursue our potential. It yearns to take us into our destiny. Mystery is the best of teachers because it knows the language of our hearts—even the mischief-filled heart of a mud-speckled six-year-old sneaking up on a frog.

*L*assie and I lunged through tangled bushes in hot pursuit of another Kermit to replace the one that had become a lump inside my snake. Mushy moss beneath calloused bare feet and cattails waving far above my head, the swamp and the forest were my favorite hideouts. Here I absconded from alien invasions consisting of the occasional shiny car purring stealthily up our long driveway bearing smelly strangers.

Visitors from the outside world rarely managed to find their way out to our homestead in the Wisconsin boondocks. I viewed them as aliens because they wore perfume that reminded me of fake flowers. In contrast, the aromas of daily life characterized my parents. The pungent odor of aircraft dope followed Dad when he worked on airplanes, or manly sweat when he dug a posthole or built a wooden shed or a rock wall. Moist earth and the crisp fragrance of vegetable leaves surrounded Mom when she worked in the garden, or in the kitchen luscious aromas of fresh bread, apple pie and pot roast.

Visitors wore shiny shoes with no holes and brightly colored blouses and pants that looked stiff and uncomfortable because they had no patches. Mom told me that far away in the concrete jungle city dwellers shopped in glitzy places called malls and paid as much as $25 for a piece of clothing. We, Mom asserted, were the smart ones, because we bought our clothes at yard sales and paid 25 cents. That suited me fine because wearing old clothes meant Mom didn't scold me for blackberry juice smeared on my shirt or skinned knees protruding through ripped pants or green stains from sliding down hills on my butt.

Our car wasn't shiny and its engine made a sound more akin to a growl than a purr. Scratches and dents decorated every inch and rust crept up on the fenders and cat fur adorned the seats. We hauled lumber on the roof and goats and chickens inside and rocks in the trunk. Dad taught me our car was better than the shiny new ones because it served so many uses.

Decades later I would discover these teachings were their strategy to shield me from feeling deprived. Our income of $400 a month did not allow for nice cars and new clothes.

Much preferred to the rigors of facing down a human other than my familiar parents, a perch high up in a pine tree with sap in my disheveled brown mop and scratches on my tawny arms joined me in blissful covenant with nature. The woods or the swamp also served as refuge, where I fled to escape the occasional well-deserved spanking.

Perpetual fascination and potential discoveries awaited me amidst rotten logs and murky waters. Caterpillars and bugs of motley sorts, dainty walking sticks, lovely butterflies, slithering snakes and slimy blue-spotted salamanders—treasures of nature that Mom had taught me to neither fear nor harm, but otherwise to enjoy. All were my friends and no day was complete until I had captured and held one of them for a few moments, if not also carried it back to my menagerie in the old steel horse trough–turned–zoo.

Senses engrossed in *missio reptilia*, I failed to notice the lengthening shadows as afternoon waned toward evening. Then I remembered . . . it must be time for the fight! With a gasp I abandoned my quest of capturing Kermits.

"Dad! Dad, it's time! Come on, let's go!" Dashing up out of the swamp and into the shop adjoining our rustic Alpine home, I clamped grimy fingers onto his hairy wrist and yanked with all forty pounds of might.

"Hey there!" Grinning, Dad lurched forward as if thrown off balance. I pulled again, then let go to see if he had apprehended my message.

He checked his watch. "Five minutes." The bristles of a wide paintbrush flexed and glistened as he daubed dope onto a strip of raw fabric freshly overlaid on an aircraft spar.

"Nooo! Come *now*!" I bounced up and down.

He dropped a lid onto the dope can and stuffed the brush into a jar of thinner. Satisfied that my battle partner was on his way, I barged into the house, homemade screen door slamming after my heels.

The house matched our car—practical. No carpet to soil but a scattering of throw rugs here and there on the flagstone floor. Yard sales were not only our source of clothing but also our source for furniture. One sofa's yellow and green speckled upholstery evoked images of a rotting orange and the other was the hue of Lassie's number two. Mom taught me that looks didn't matter since the sofas served their purpose of providing a soft destination for weary posteriors.

Nevertheless, I now faced a serious hurdle: crossing the minefield and dodging the bullets without being hit. Legs spinning faster than the Road Runner, I dashed through the kitchen and into the living room with all the speed I could muster. To no avail. Mom's voice tagged me from behind. "Wash your feet. You're tracking mud everywhere. And scrub your hands with soap, please. We'll have no frog pee or snake excrement at the dinner table!"

I skidded to a stop. Mom's leniency regarding stained clothes didn't extend into uncleanliness, and failure to respond when spoken to served as ample ground for a tanning. Even so, the "Okay" I threw over my shoulder while flying back out the door carried no intention of complete obedience. One leap into the duck pond and the mud vanished, replaced by speckles of green slime up to my waist. But precious seconds had been lost. The fight was on!

Back inside, a glance revealed Mom was no longer a threat since she had returned to her frying pan. I blitzed through the living room shouting back, "Feet squeaky clean, I'll wash my hands after we cream the Nazis!"

Slap, slap, slap, my wet feet pounded up the stairs and into the cockpit of the military submarine—a closet. There a steel pipe protruded down through the ragged insulation of the unfinished ceiling.

I waited, listening.

Below, the screen door banged. Dad had entered the house.

Filling my lungs I bellowed, "Enemies sighted today or not?"

Silence. No, not quite. He was talking with Mom.

I gasped. Wasting time! What could be more urgent than the imminent battle?

"*Dad!*" My yell bounced back off the rough exposed two-by-fours framing the interior of the closet. Self-taught architects, Dad and Mom had designed and built the house from the ground up, but practicality alone mattered to them. Upon reaching the final stage of adding finishing touches, their impetus ebbed. Thus our interior walls remained brown paper stapled to uprights with yellow insulation protruding around the edges and some portion of the words "Rock Wall" or "Gold Bond" repeated every two feet.

"Yeah, coming." His voice wafted up a little nearer to directly below me. He had made it to the living room.

"Are there enemies? Is the coast clear?"

No sound. Then, from beneath the floorboards under my feet, "Aw, crap!"

As expected. It would be a fight today. Planting my toes, I stretched my fingers around the pipe. Ready for action! Any minute and I would fire away.

"Aim . . . a little south," hollered Dad.

Gripping the pipe with both wee fists, I strained. With a creaking, grating groan of steel against wood, the gigantic antenna atop our roof rotated.

Dad's instructions floated up from below. "Keep going . . . keep going . . . whoa!"

I reversed forces to halt the rotation and bolted to the top of the stairs. "Okay? Did we nab 'em?"

"Nope. Go the other way."

I cranked on the pipe again. Back the antenna swung, this time slowly in a full circle.

"Okay, stop there."

"Killed 'em?"

No answer.

To the stairwell again. Below, Dad's voice resembled a growling pit bull. Mumbling to himself. Not happy.

"Which way should I turn it?"

No answer. I could tell he was fiddling with the dials. Then he sounded the dreaded "Aaaahhhhgh! No use."

We and our antenna had lost the battle against prevailing precipitation and atmospheric disturbance. I hurled myself down the stairs. Sure enough. Obnoxious, relentless snow obscured 70 percent of the picture.

Not to be deterred, albeit with crooked faces, we settled down to watch our show, straining to see and hear through the snow and static that squawked out of the twelve-inch black-and-white set.

This was Dad's and my ritual. Four thirty p.m. Monday through Friday marked our time to shout and cheer and roll with laughter watching Hogan and his troop of POWs make monkeys out of Sergeant Schultz and Colonel Klink. The cunning acumen of running a secret espionage unit smack in the middle of enemy territory triggered my fascination, and a secret crush on Hogan intensified matters. Through the smokescreen of childish reasoning he appeared in some episodes to put himself in harm's way to protect his men or to accomplish the mission.

Hogan's Heroes exceeded entertainment. Though hidden at the time, Mystery cast a shadow on my future, which would revolve around two passions: love and conquest. Love of a radically different kind, and an impossible conquest into the darkest regions of the planet.

In 1969—a year before I entered the world—Dad and Mom acquired forty acres of 90 percent swamp at an auction for the winning bid of $516.36. Thieves stole their chain saw so they hewed a space for the house like the old-time pioneers—with an ax. From Mom's drafting skills and Dad's architectural prowess rose a lovely Alpine chalet with flagstone flooring and rockwork up to the scalloped red fascia crowning the eaves. Then Dad hacked farther through the forest until he had cleared himself a "patch" in which none but he and a few of his advanced flying students could put down a plane. They dubbed the homestead/airport "Hawk's Haven."

According to Dad's flying buddies, Hawk's Haven's address was "you can't get there from here." Living out in the sticks has its drawbacks, and years passed before I experienced the wonder of telephones and light bulbs. My parents deemed neither of sufficient necessity to afford the $1,800 it would have cost to bring power lines through the wilderness to the homestead. Oak and maple logs fueled the cookstove, and the refrigerator ran on propane. The TV was powered by storage batteries recharged by a noisy generator that lived in the shop along with Dad's half-finished airplane fuselages.

Propane lighting fixtures adorned the walls. Inside each glass globe a little whitish sock covered a porcelain base. When the shadows grew long, Mom turned a steel key at the base of the globe and stuck a match inside, and the sock began to glow. After a few moments encroaching shadows retreated and the room became a little brighter than dark.

Life was sweet and filled with joys—savoring the steaming butter-lavished heel of homemade bread just pulled from the oven, riding Pony Boy while Mom walked alongside singing and joining Lassie in romps through radiant meadows carpeted with Indian paintbrushes. Chewing the honeysuckles that pushed out of the dense forest on either side of the runway yielded a dainty sweetness, but the sorrow of causing such a lovely flower to sacrifice itself for my taste buds counterbalanced the pleasure.

Tight finances and ragged clothes didn't keep my parents from raising me to believe myself a queen. Dad could be boisterous at times, but I was his shining star and he made sure I knew it. In the summer Dad took me to swim in the lake, and in the fall we wrestled in great mounds of dry leaves. In winter he took me racing about on the snowmobile or engaged me in snowball fights. When the weather warmed he pushed me on the swing he had suspended from a tree limb and let me knock him down with my feet.

But one vivid memory of Dad, emblazoned as a brand seared into my anima, stands as a cornerstone of my identity. Gripping my shoulders, his brown eyes looking deep into mine, he would say with gruff fatherly love, *"Don't ever let anybody tell you you can't do something. You can do anything you want to if you wanna do it bad enough."* This mantra, coupled with his and Mom's demonstration of industrious can-do independence, inspired me to grow up fearless and dauntless, believing that the word *impossible* did not exist.

My friends were boys because the boys liked my swamp and my woods and weren't scared of my snakes and frogs. They joined in scaling the sky-piercing pines and seeing how far we could walk on the swamp's fallen logs before toppling into the quagmire. Girls bored me. Their aspirations extended no further than a tame bedroom and a boxful of dollies and teacups. My first and last baby doll met her end the day I hurled her up into the tree branches and eventually succeeded in stringing her up by the hair. An insatiable quest for adventure undergirded every waking moment, propelling me in rollicking revelry to find new impediments of which to show myself master.

But there was more. Mystery called to me, a voice unheard, a force unseen, unexplainable. A longing. A crying. It tugged at me from deep within.

On summer nights I slept on the screened-in porch. Beyond the porous barricade hummed a voracious squadron of blood-seeking insects, frustrated at their prey being so near and yet inaccessible. Rain pitter-pattering on the oak and maple leaves bobbed them up and down inches from my face. The aroma of damp forest wafted across my bed, enfolding me in paradisaical bliss. A stronger gust carried a fine mist onto my skin, the pristine kiss of nature.

Clear, cool weather offered the possibility of the most intense nocturnal delight—a meeting between that deep-down mysterious cry and my favorite sound of all. On those rare, precious nights, at first far away, then as luck might ordain closer and stronger, an enchanting sound pierced the forest.

"*Whip-poor-will! Whip-poor-will!*"

The song of a night bird wasn't all I heard. The voice penetrated my soul more vividly than my eardrums. At the call of the whip-poor-will a chill of ecstasy tremored through my body and a strange longing rose up inside. The whip-poor-will spoke its language, resonated with it and gave words to the movements deep within for which I could find no expression. "A treasure awaits!" sang the whip-poor-will. "A great treasure, concealed in darkness, terrible but lovely. It's far away over the treetops. Deep into the night. It's calling you. Follow me and I'll take you there."

But I could not follow the whip-poor-will. I could only listen to its beckon and gaze up into the treetops, black against the moonlit sky. What treasure? The mystery and intrigue of it tormented me with a lovely longing and excitement combined with a twinge of innate foreboding.

For where treasure lies, dragons also lurk.

Buried in the center of my soul, another voice whispered, "The day is coming when you will follow. Soon you will enter the dread adventure."

From beneath a spread newspaper protruded half-unlaced boots propped up on the coffee table. "Stupid SOBs." Dad flipped the page with enough vehemence to tear it.

"What's 'a matter, honey?" queried Mom, seated at her treadle sewing machine across the room.

"The schools around here ought'a be called whorehouses!"

"I knew they were crummy." Mom lifted the foot, snipped the thread and draped a half-stitched pair of pants across the Singer. She drew near and peered over his shoulder.

Dad turned back to the page. "Look here." He leveled a finger encased in dry aircraft dope from his day's work. "It says the school Leanna's s'posed to start attending this fall has the highest rate of VD in the state! There ain't no way we're sending her there!"

Mom straightened. "I guess that confirms we're teaching her ourselves."

Dad jerked and closed the paper with a sudden rustle. "What? Keep her out of school?"

"Well," declared Mom, "nowadays more and more parents teach their own kids."

Dad swiveled around and cast a dubious glance over the top of his five-dollar drugstore specs. "You gave the bird to yer college professor and I flew the coop in fifth grade. What do you propose we're going to teach her?"

But neither of my parents were your typical dropouts. Both had chosen to buck the system, pursue their dreams in a hostile world and prove that the word *impossible* does not exist.

Rewind to the year 1930, when Dad was a schoolboy.

The teacher's voice droned on in harmony with bees gathering pollen from the first flowers of spring. Beyond the window of the one-room schoolhouse a farmer labored over his plough, shouting an occasional command at two plodding mules. Thus a balmy afternoon in northern Pennsylvania rolled lazily by.

"Now, read it together." Miss Moore tapped the blackboard with her chalk.

"Jimmy . . . runs . . . fast. Mary . . . eats . . . lunch," chanted a chorus of fifth graders.

"Who can tell me the subject of the first sentence? . . . Yes, Susie?"

A rosy-cheeked wench in a frilly plaid dress chirped, "The subject is 'Jimmy.'"

"Good. And the verb?"

"The verb is 'run.'"

"Excellent." Miss Moore's attention shifted to a boy seated near the window. Adjusting round spectacles, her eyes narrowed. "Joseph, what are you doing?"

The lad jumped as if poked by an invisible goad. *Thunk!* He clapped a book shut. "Studying, ma'am."

"Studying what?"

Ragged trousers and toes protruding from worn-out, undersized sneakers pegged him to be the son of impoverished Italian immigrants, but the dissentive independence with which he met the teacher's gaze suggested a kindred spirit with Huck Finn or Tom Sawyer. "English, ma'am."

The boy across from Joe stifled a snicker. *Jane's All the World's Aircraft* included no chapter on sentence structure.

"If you were studying English, why did you close the book when I spoke to you?" queried Miss Moore.

With exceptional poise Joe answered, "Because instead of studying the English book I should have been answering your questions, ma'am." As a hasty afterthought, he added, "Oh, and . . . I'm sorry, too."

Miss Moore eyed him askance. "You're sorry. Really?"

"Yes, ma'am."

The teacher sighed. "Well, okay, I'll accept that. . . . So what is the verb in the second sentence, Joseph?"

Joe's face drained to ashen, dismay supplanting his prior fortitude.

"The verb, Joseph?"

"Uhhh . . . runs."

"The second sentence, not the first."

A long silence. He stared at the board. "Lunch."

Hushed giggles rippled through the class. Miss Moore glowered at Joe. "The verb, class?"

Several hands shot skyward.

"Eats."

"Correct. Now, who will make a sentence and tell us the subject and the verb? Four of you, come to the board and write a sentence. Quickly now . . ."

Not daring to open his airplane book again, Joe twirled a pencil between his fingers. His eyes drifted out the window. A bird soared overhead, dipping and rising on warm eddies. Effortless, it hung in the middle of the blue heavens, each feather a pianist's finger, pinioned Mozart playing the wind, music in flight. *One day I'll be up there, too,* he mused.

Far in the distance a sound wafted to his ears. For a moment Joe thought a bumblebee might have found its way into the schoolhouse. Then he knew it wasn't a bee, but . . . an airplane! A mile from the schoolhouse lay a little grassy airstrip where every so often a plane landed.

By the height of the sun Joe knew school didn't let out for another hour. In a few minutes the plane would land and he would miss the action!

The sound of the engine hummed closer and closer. *A Cub . . . no, maybe an Aeronca . . .* He could picture the airplane, the pilot . . . but here he sat, stuck in this school building, this . . . prison! The sweet reek of engine oil awakened his senses like Vicks. The whirring prop pushed a hurricane-force wind through his thick dark hair.

Desperate, he glanced about the room. The teacher was engrossed in her lesson. Oblivious to the approaching plane, his classmates belted corrections and suggestions while their peers scratched sentences on the board.

Mystery summoned Joe to his destiny. The drumming engine transported his mind out of the classroom. His hands touched the smooth fabric, fondled the molded wood of the

43

prop, caressed the glistening spinner. The room began to fade. Leathery face beaming, the pilot stepped down from the cockpit. Goggles formed frog eyes atop a snug brown cap pulled over his ears.

Joe strode forward. "Good afternoon, sir!" The pilot gazed down at him with a look that asked, *Why aren't you in school, kid?*

But Joe was not to be deterred. "Sir, how do you control the plane? Please show me." Now the pilot knew. He looked past the schoolboy to the dream beyond, the mystery of the skies beating in Joe's heart. With a grin the pilot stepped back into the cockpit and pushed a lever. As if by magic the ailerons and rudders swiveled up and down, up and down. . . .

Joe snapped back to reality. The window! He peeped over at it. Barely three feet from his shoulder. The shutter already half-open. He calculated the sequence of moves—the exit from his desk, the leap, the push and the tumble to freedom . . . but what if Miss Moore caught him? Last time his hands were black and blue before she had finished beating him with the ruler.

"This sentence has a grammatical error." Miss Moore scanned the class, tapping her chalk on the board. "Who can find the error?"

With the intense fixation of a cat waiting to pounce on a mouse, Joe watched and waited. Her back, not her face, must be classward before he made his move.

Hands raised. Miss Moore nodded.

An obedient student piped, "The dog barks loudly, not loud."

"Yes, very good!" Miss Moore swiveled toward the blackboard and Joe saw his chance. Tucking the airplane book under an arm, he sprang out of the desk in such a rush the desk scooted sideways. Steel feet grated on wooden floor-boards. His intent no longer a secret, sixty eyes turned on him.

"Joseph! What are you doing?" shouted Miss Moore.

But Joe wasn't turning back now. "Airplane!" tumbled from his lips. With one deft shove, the shutter banged open. Careless for what might lie below, he plunged through head-first, landing on his back in the weeds and rocks.

Miss Moore's voice followed him. "Joseph! You come back here! Come back here right now!" The sound of her enraged cries waned. His legs propelled him across the field in the direction of his mystery and his dream.

In 1935 jobs were hard to come by, but Joe had a dream and a will to pursue it. At fifteen years of age, without a penny in his pocket, Joe hoboed to reach the headquarters of Piper Aircraft. Under his arm he carried a shoe box. Inside the shoe box rested Joe's hope of a job: a model airplane made of balsa wood. Thanks to his study of aerodynamics combined with an innate engineering aptitude, he had so perfectly adjusted the model that on the power of a wound-up rubber band it took off, circled around and landed at his feet.

Mr. Piper was so impressed he gave him a job building aircraft wings. But Joe still didn't know how to fly and had no money for lessons. So he smuggled enough materials to build his own plane, and then taught himself to fly. Despite the odds, he had attained his dream. During WWII his aeronautical skills landed him the illustrious but potentially lethal post as one of five elite fighter pilots. All were eventually shot down while conducting over-the-shoulder bombing raids. Joe and one other survived.

After the war Joe and his brother built a restaurant called the Matterhorn below the flatirons near Boulder.

My mom, Kathy, had a dream, too. During her teenage years she loved to lie on her back in the grass gazing up at the sky. "One day I'll be up there, flying like a bird," she mused. But reality carried her on the path toward becoming a teacher. When she commented that the material in the textbook made no rational sense, the B.Ed. professor replied, "I know it, but don't rock the boat. I want my tenure."

Disgusted, she walked out. "I can't be true to myself and also blindly learn and teach compromise and nonsense," she reasoned.

One day she drove past the Matterhorn and noticed a little plane sitting out back. The newly opened restaurant was hiring. Motivated not so much by economics as by her hope to score a ride in the plane, she donned her most chic outfit and applied. Within days Joe took the new waitress/hot babe for a spin in his plane, and then taught her to fly.

Horrified that their daughter had fallen in love with an uneducated immigrant twenty years her senior, Kathy's parents rejected their proposition of marriage. Soon afterward, with dismantled airplane strapped to the roof of a 1940 Chrysler, they left Colorado. Alerting neither family nor friends of their intentions, they set out to find adventure.

Joe had been married before the war, but while he bombed Nazis she had absconded with their child. Embittered and guesstimating that the fiercely independent Kathy might do likewise, he declined to father a child. When Kathy threatened to dump him unless he gave her a baby, he consented.

The day after my birth, Joe declared, "I suppose we should make a trip to the courthouse." In an era when children born out of wedlock were considered a matter for shame, I entered the world.

A Secret Romance

Mom and Dad were not hesitant to buck social systems that violated the moral values and freedom they cherished. Observing the dismal standards of morality in the public schools, they determined their daughter would not be thus contaminated. In 1975, however, homeschooling was illegal in most states. After contemplating going head-to-head with the government, they realized their incarceration wouldn't have been of particular benefit to me. So rather than contend with the law, they chose to quit Wisconsin.

The monthly issue of *Mother Earth News* arrived, and Mom discovered a want ad for a caretaker to live on and look after a future campground in Arivaca, Arizona. Located in one of the few states that allowed homeschooling and promising the opposite climate from Wisconsin's six months of deep freeze, the offer looked appealing.

But Dad was pessimistic. Through a slurp of freshly brewed "gas," he growled, "Where's Arivaca, smack in the middle of Satan's den?"

Mom made a face. "In the middle of *what*?"

"That megapolis . . . heck, what's the big city down there?" Dad operated under the following rule: If the sound of another homo sapien or device made by a homo sapien could be detected, the locale was too congested. "There's a house behind every tree nowadays," he complained. So wherever we moved, it would have to be "out in the sticks" again.

A call to the owner verified that the campground consisted of a rural patch of mesquite trees with a dry wash through the middle and a trailer house. Seventy-five miles removed from "Satan's den"—Tucson—it satisfied Dad's requirements.

Arizona posed a whole new corpus of adventures for a mischievous rascal. Discovering a plenteous supply of wild gourds, I persuaded my new friends to smash them and do battle with gourd guts as ammo. Hot afternoons brought a herd of free-ranging Brahma bulls to stand under the shade trees by the pond. From safely behind our newly erected four-strand barbed-wire fence, I dared to tease them. Lassie #2 easily fell for my insidious invitation to maul the poisonous toads I proffered on my palm. She promptly spit them out and ran frothing for water.

Our two-door Dodge Dart vaguely resembled the General Lee in my now-favorite show, *The Dukes of Hazzard*. I determined neither to enter nor exit except in the fashion of my new crush, Bo, and his cousin, Luke. Whether parallel-parked along a curb or visiting friends, my ever-patient parents quietly endured while their undignified daughter exited the car by climbing through the window and sprawling headfirst on the ground.

After a year Dad succumbed to sunstroke, and we determined Arizona was too hot.

Missouri's climate fared halfway between hot and cold, and homeschooling was allowed. We bought forty acres of mountain and built our house from the ground up with our own hands. In the meantime we lived in a shack tacked together with two-by-fours and tar paper. Off in the brush Dad and Mom dug a hole in the ground and set a toilet seat over it. A protruding branch served as toilet paper holder. A little ways farther into the woods, three trees happened to grow closely together. Enclosed with a strip of plastic, this became our shower stall for private bucket baths.

Missouri brought more adventure. There were bedrock creeks up which to gallop my pony, trees full of rotting persimmons to smear on Lassie and an old hillbilly thief up the road who stole our best puppy of the litter. Having studied the American Indians in homeschooling class, I decided that if a young brave could slide down around his galloping pony and grab things from near the ground, so could I. Thus every afternoon my pony and I tore up and down the meadow with Lassie bringing up the rear.

Chiggers proved Missouri's sole but significant shortcoming. At night we had to bathe in Clorox water to assuage the tormentous itching that drew blood.

Winter arrived with blustery weather and ice storms. Though still unfinished, the new house was warm and snug. With the exception of the bathroom, interior walls didn't exist. Kitchen, living room and bedrooms merged together in a single rectangular space. My bed consisted of a mattress on the floor since the bedsprings were still packed away. When my nine o'clock bedtime came, I learned to go to sleep serenaded by the *clink-clink* of Mom washing dishes, along with her and Dad's muted voices as they attempted to avoid disturbing me. I learned to go to sleep in fairly broad daylight since it was much later when lights-out and silence signaled they, too, had turned in. Not yet covered by drywall, a few inches from my cheek the brown backing of fiberglass insulation bulged out between two studs. Occasionally a spider or centipede peeked around the edge, happy to have found a new home.

But my little corner wasn't lonely and the spider and centipede were not my sole companions. Having no shop, Dad's airplane projects shared the house with us. The metal skeleton of a wing dangled by ropes from a beam in the ceiling above my head. Two wooden horses paralleled my bed and supported a spar. The carpet on the untiled plywood floor changed daily.

Sawdust today, metal scraps tomorrow and wood chips interspersed with an occasional screw, nail or tool. These remnants of Dad's sawing and cutting and sanding routinely made their way onto my blanket and into bed with me.

Mystery anticipates those moments when our busyness has abated, allowing us to hear its whisper. Mystery leads us upward, outward, beyond ourselves. It takes us into uncharted lands and shows us wonders to come and ancient wisdom long buried. But in our human frailty, we rarely understand what we're seeing.

Until now, I had glimpsed the shadow of Mystery in nature, heard its call in the whip-poor-will's song and flowed with its tug in my ceaseless quest for adventure. But now Mystery would open to me a wide cavern of absolute wonder.

It began one night when I lay down to sleep. Darkly at first then with increasing clarity, a movie began to play behind my eyelids. Neither my thoughts nor my imagination gave rise to the action. It just happened, independent of my mind.

Then I was swept into it. The airplane wing over my head, the spider, the mutterings of my parents across the room melted away. I lost awareness of my arms and legs and whether I was lying down or standing.

I was no longer Leanna, but a girl named Talwyn in an exotic world where mountains hung from the sky and everyone could fly. Humans who had come here from Earth coexisted peacefully with a motley of exotic native creatures whose nonverbal speech I understood clearly as plain English.

The experience lasted an hour, and then it began to fade. For long moments afterward I lay gazing out at the stars, speechless, wondering in awe at what had happened.

The following night I brushed my teeth and yanked on my jammies and crawled into bed full of suspense. Would I again be transported into that wondrous world? Sure enough. Soon after lying down, eyes open and fully awake, I began to drift, transiting out of myself, out of my earthly life and into that other realm. I hadn't read C. S. Lewis, but akin to the children in the wardrobe, my bed framed a doorway between worlds.

This time I learned that all was not well in this otherwise paradisaical world. An unknown force was ambushing those traveling here from Earth. Weeping and mourning now raked a dark smear across a land that hitherto had known perpetual joy.

Then, too soon it faded again. I found myself on my bed, gazing up at the ceiling, mind aswirl with the pain I'd seen on the faces of bereaved humans and their native friends. Together we grieved for those who had, by all appearances, been abducted by a dreadful deep-space marauder.

Immersive and vivid, the experience swept me into a second life. Nevertheless I remained in full control of my senses. Talwyn could return into Leanna at will. Each night the drama resumed at the time and place where the previous had ended and I lived another episode in the cosmic serial. Some nights featured reruns, and I enjoyed them the second and third time as intensely as the first. After a few repeats, the narrative proceeded onward. The conclusion of each left me desperately anticipating the next. Tomorrow night was an unbearably long time for which to wait, and bedtime became the most exciting part of my day.

Having rollicked for millennia in a harmonious utopia, the native creatures in my nighttime life had no concept of war. A band of scouts set out to retrace the path from which the travelers had disappeared. When they also failed to return, the season of peaceful coexistence with whatever was out there ended.

Defense council meetings were called to order, and a young man revealed new intelligence on the enemy. With sober resolve he pledged to "break the power of the darkness." He was plain, unassuming, even gentle in countenance and lean of stature—a demeanor more befitting of a Van Gogh than a military commander.

At first I, as Talwyn, disdained him. Brawn and clout and shrewd schemes and iron will I perceived to be the stuff of heroes, and since by appearances this man embodied none of those, his ambitious vow struck me as ludicrous.

To join his mission the man selected two majestic horselike creatures. Then, despite my unconcealed scorn, he chose me. The king of the land endowed us with magical powers. Thus was born "The Team." We embarked upon daring forays into deep space and traveled to strange planets.

The reader may reasonably assume that popular sci-fi flicks in vogue during those years inspired my experiences. However, in the sheltered and remote rural life my parents had chosen, I did not so much as know that *Star Trek* or *Star Wars* existed and I hadn't viewed a single episode.

The Team's expeditions brought us up against dreadful creatures, and beyond enemy lines we discovered miserable captives slogging in labor camps or rotting in prisons. We fought vicious battles, suffered countless wounds and endured terrifying hardships, but in the end, we succeeded in rescuing the captives and escorting them safely home. Death posed no threat as we were immortal. However, of constant and grave concern, to fall into enemy hands would doom us to an eternity of unknown terrors.

The action and adventure would not have in itself captivated me night after night. The exotic creatures we fought and the thrill of victory were not what compelled me. Even the compassion and sorrow I felt for the ragged captives and the jubilation at seeing the sparkle of life return to their wizened faces at their first taste of freedom, fell short. None of these drove my yearning to return over and over into that world.

An element completely other is that which held me positively spellbound. It overwhelmed me with awe and filled my heart to bursting with a gentle, quiet but fervid love—the man who had chosen me to accompany him on this great task.

Through the trials and rigors of our mission, my prior image of the man had reversed. I began to see into his heart. I discovered there a mysterious radiance, a strength like iron driven by love of the purest kind. His loveliness eclipsed all creation and every other being in the cosmos. His buoyant personality irradiated everything around him with the light of a midday sun. In serious moments his demeanor exuded humble authority rendering chastened the wagging tongue. His presence lifted the lowest worm to the status of royal guest and made impossibilities possible. To look into his eyes was to be drawn into pools of profound wisdom and enveloped in ineffable, self-effacing love. When he laid his hand on my shoulder, a chill tingled through my body, engulfing me in unbearable ecstasy.

Mine was the undeserved privilege and unspeakable romance of partnership with this extraordinary person. Nearness to him epitomized the fulfillment of my ultimate ambition.

The man exceeded the definition of a hero. Out in enemy realms the battle at times grew so ferocious, and we were so grievously wounded as to arrive at the brink of despair. Fearing capture ourselves, the horses and I desired to abandon the prisoners and escape. In those dark moments, bloody and barely able to stand, the man had stopped fighting long enough to look us in the eyes. Oblivious to his own pain he cried, "We can't leave without the citizens! We have to rescue them!" Then he threw himself into the thickest part of the battle. His courage and devotion to freeing the hapless prisoners imbued us with new strength and determination. Because of his leadership, our excursions invariably culminated in victory, and we never failed to return home with a troop of freed captives.

Yet a deeper mystery cloaked him in alluring enigma. A secret lay buried in his heart, a profound and inscrutable piece of knowledge that he declined to divulge. I glimpsed it when we were back home resting. He would go off alone and be lost in deep thought. At those times I saw a strain and a heaviness in his face and his perpetual smile momentarily faded into—could it be—fear?

To my "What's wrong?" he replied with esoteric reserve, "I have to break the power of the darkness." Chiding him for thinking in the singular, I assured him we were in this fight together. But he would not be comforted. He responded to my reasonings with silence. At last I could only sit by him, hold him in my arms and wonder what lay ahead.

For lack of appropriate descriptive words, I dubbed my nighttime life "The Dream."

I told no one of The Dream. My parents at best would brush it off as a childish fantasy. At worst they might tragically mistake my adventure for mental infirmity and subject me to a psychiatrist. But a far greater reason inspired me to keep The Dream secret. Down in the abyss of my soul, I knew my experience contained a truth that transcended this world. My life brimmed with a rich medley of joys and adventures. But the multiplicity of splendors mingled into one could not approach the beauty of the man in The Dream. Occupying a deserted corner of my vocabulary lived a word I hadn't yet understood—the word *holy*.

In Mom's bookshelf lived a dusty black leather volume. On its spine inscribed in gold letters were the words *Holy Bible*. I knew *Bible* had something to do with God and *holy* meant something beyond human. I didn't know where I might meet God, and though my parents were good and perhaps even great people, they most certainly didn't qualify as holy.

But now for the first time I understood. The lovely man in The Dream was holy. Therefore The Dream was holy. Though the ability to explain why and how escaped me, I knew The Dream embodied a reality utterly precious, more priceless than the fairest diamond, more desirable than the highest joy or pleasure life can offer. The Dream was my personal treasure, my cherished and jealously guarded secret.

Mystery led me on. I now soared over the treetops. The dread wonder promised in the whip-poor-will's call surely lay just over my horizon, on the threshold ready to burst into view.

Agates

After a year my parents had endured their fill of Missouri's chiggers and ice storms. Back in Arizona, Mom engaged her drafting board to design a partially subterranean abode offering natural air-conditioning.

The equine species had won out over all my hobbies and now enjoyed a monopoly of my leisure time. But when selecting a mount, my parents went heavy on emotion and light on wisdom. In my eight years of life I'd gone through six different ponies. Typically after the pony sent me for a few undignified sprawls into the brambles or the mud, my parents sold it and tried again. My current pony—a green-broke palomino—had racked up a criminal record that included running through a barbed-wire fence with the buggy, bucking me off when I tried to ride him bareback and pitching Mom off and breaking her scapula. Determined to acquire a well-trained pony for a change, Mom and Dad scraped together $1,000 and we trekked to northern California. There we bought a professionally trained purebred Welch.

Dad named the red chestnut mare Contento, translated "happiness" in Italian. Though she usually lived up to her name, Contento persisted in a particularly unladylike habit. When bored with chewing on dry mesquite beans or rummaging in the dirt for remnants of hay, she made sport of cornering other horses in the three-sided shed and mercilessly pummeling them with both rear hooves. Desperate squealing and hooves thudding on hide cued me to snatch the buggy whip kept handy for this express purpose and sprint for the paddock. Charging to the rescue of the terrified victim and scoring maximum whacks on the female bully's retreating hindquarters stimulated a sensation of intense pleasure.

One evening I ventured beyond the back boundary of our property, into Brahma bull territory. There, scattered on the ground, lay whitish objects. Had the location been anywhere north of Arizona and the weather significant degrees colder, I would have assumed them to be globs of snow.

White agates!

Agates I had glimpsed in trinket shops but to happen upon pure white ones held par with a lottery jackpot. Translucent lines and crystals weren't all they offered. Swirls of lava, frozen in place umpteen years ago, whisked me into the past, my own personal time machine. I had discovered a gold mine of wonder! Elated, I hauled back a whole bucket full of them.

Thus commenced a craze that persisted well into my teens. The majority of agates featured my favorite color, a deep chestnut brown. A royal crown of pure crystals graced their center. Under the gaze of a novice, unbroken agates appear as one more worthless rock, but the agate virtuoso can spy the telltale geodic shape from a distance. Drawing nearer, my eye could detect the hint of translucency in the rough, dirty gray-brown surface. Whether traversing a gravel road, climbing a hill or even crossing a paved highway, my eyes were inseparably riveted to the ground in hopes of finding an agate, causing my parents to fear for my sanity.

Upon sighting a rock that might be an agate, my friends and I snatched it up and dashed home. With the intensity of a team of surgeons in an emergency room we prepared to conduct the delicate operation of cracking our specimen. Placing our find inside a rag to avoid losing a precious fragment, we began to tap it with a hammer, lightly at first, then steadily harder, until it cracked open. Then crawling over one another with anticipation, we pressed in to discover whether a dazzling wonder lay within. Most often drab gray stone greeted us with disappointment. But on rare occasions, upon folding back the tattered cloth and brushing away the debris from the newly cracked stone, we were rewarded with a treasure. Our eyes were the first ever to behold the pristine lines and sparkling crystals now liberated from centuries of dark entombment.

My hoarding of agates transcended the definition of a hobby. Possessing an agate meant holding in my hand a little piece of mystery. Hidden for centuries and now discovered and first glimpsed by me, the crystals echoed the call of the whip-poor-will. *"There's more! The Mystery lives! Look deeper. The treasure waits to be found!"* The glint and gleam of each dainty crystal beckoned, *"There's something precious hidden deep, deep in the darkness. Come inside and find it!"* The translucent swirls were 3-D. I could stare into them forever and their depth swept me away, paths leading me into the agate, into the mystery, into the darkness to find the hidden treasure, to rescue the ragged crystal and bring it into the light so it could shine.

But what exactly was this yearning deep in my soul? What did I long for? A wee voice whispered, *"The Dream holds the answer."* So night after night with ardent anticipation I jumped into bed and portaled into my other life. There the lovely man and I and the two mighty horses discovered new worlds, battled monsters and set captives free. There, night after night, I was enraptured and captivated by the gentle power and selfless gallantry of the man.

Mom worked as a waitress at night while by day Dad earned a little income by selling and installing windmills to pump water for the ranchers. A tireless worker and immovably stubborn, he refused to join the locals in their routine siesta. One afternoon he returned home complaining of a splitting headache. Mom made him a bed on the couch with an ice-cold lemonade and a cool, damp washrag on his forehead. But the pain in his head intensified and he grew dizzy.

At last he muttered, "Take me to the hospital."

Dad going to the hospital! The five-foot-four-inch giant who could outlift and outrun six-footers half his age, reduced to going to a hospital! Until that day the sensation of fear had been foreign to me, but I couldn't muster the courage to ask Mom the question pounding in my heart—"Is Daddy going to die?"

Mom's ashen, expressionless face offered no comfort. "Open the door!" she ordered as she helped Dad outside. Then, gripping the handle of the car door, I watched her help Dad ease into the passenger side and perched on the edge of the backseat while Mom drove to the hospital.

Mom and I stayed overnight on a couch in a waiting room while Dad received treatment. He had succumbed to sunstroke before, but this was now the third time. In the morning he was okay, but the doctor cautioned, "You can't work in the heat, and you have to live in an air-conditioned house."

"I'll be fine," Dad countered in his gruff, independent way. "Let's go home." But as soon as the hot rays of the sun licked the top of his head, the searing pain recurred, forcing us to pull off the road and take refuge in an air-conditioned restaurant. There my parents made the difficult decision that we would have to leave Arizona for good.

In the cool of the night, we strapped Dad's dismantled airplane onto the roof of the car, loaded the ponies into the trailer and set out. Most of our belongings had to stay behind. I lay on a mattress in the back of the cutout Dodge Dart, looking up at the stars and wondering where we were going this time.

We ended up in the state of Washington. An old dilapidated house under the trees served as home. Our living room had a hill in the middle where water had leaked through the roof, swelling the floorboards until they buckled upward. It didn't take long for us to learn that in Washington, it's not a good idea to live among the trees. The dreary drizzle, relentless as the sun in Arizona, ensured that no material object ever dried. A watery world of perpetual dampness subsumed the ground, the leaves and the fuzzy green mold growing on the walls *inside* the house. Laundry weighed on the sagging line for days and stank of mildew. Little green bits of guck constantly fell from above—worms and pieces of mossy tree bark and dark green bug poop.

Washington offered one more grand adventure and introduced me to a new and fascinating creature—slugs. Up to six inches in length, the nocturnal gastropods left their glistening trail of slime crisscrossing the roads. Rising early, I scooped up the fattest and juiciest I could find. Back at my desk, I sliced it open with my dissection knife. Engaging the microscope kit Dad and Mom had given me on my ninth birthday, I prepared slides smeared with various elements of internal organs and external slime, and with gusto I delved into the fascinating cellular realm.

Mom and Dad hastily procured what they considered upgraded living conditions—a camper trailer whose total length measured twelve feet. We parked our new house in a pasture near a run-down barn behind the county airstrip. Though Number One could be dispensed with behind a gravel mound, we discharged the business of Number Two and showers by taking a stroll across the airport to the public facilities. Dad earned a little money teaching flying and Mom waitressed. Their combined income still totaled around $400 a month, but it sufficed thanks to a prudential and austere lifestyle. After school my friends invariably elected to play at "Leanna's house" instead of their own. When it came to fun, plush carpets, fenced-in yards and manicured lawns were no match for ponies, airplanes, bows and arrows, a trampoline and exotic pets set in a kid's heaven of mud, briars and gravel mountains. After treating them to riding lessons on my ponies, I collected payment in the currency of thrills by terrorizing them with my reptiles.

To Fly Like a Bird

Following Kathy's first flight in Joe's little plane at the Matterhorn, the address of their favorite dating hangout became "three thousand feet in the sky." After soloing and eloping with her pilot boyfriend, Kathy had her share of hair-raising flying adventures. Now, at nine, their daughter had reached the age of initiation. Perks of Dad's service as flight instructor included free use of the airport's Citabria, Champ and Cub, so early mornings before the school bus arrived we took a "trip around the patch."

The two-seater tail draggers stood in a row at the edge of the grassy airstrip. Dad usually chose the Citabria as my lesson plane. Too little to help, I watched him reach up under the wings and untie the ropes tethering the plane to the ground. Then he opened the cockpit door and lifted me up. I stood on the metal step and peered in at the panel of dials and switches. Dad pointed to a switch with a red circle around its base. "Flip the ignition on." I pushed the switch up and a red light glowed. "Now, hop down and stand back, I'm gonna crank 'er up!"

I ran toward the tail of the plane while Dad reached up high and grabbed one blade of the prop and pulled it down hard. With the second or third crank, the engine roared to life and the prop disappeared in a whirring blur. The wind from it threatened to bowl me off my feet and the roar rendered verbal communication almost impossible.

Dad motioned for me to come forward under the wing, making sure I stayed a safe distance from the prop. The plane contained two seats, one in front of the other. Dad placed three cushions under me and two behind me and I climbed into the second seat. He fastened the heavy buckle and pulled the army-green nylon strap snug.

"Okay," he bellowed over the din of the engine. "Remember where the throttle is?"

I pointed to a black knob on the left side.

"Rudder?"

I stretched my legs forward and pushed the pedals.

"Good." Looking hard into my face, he said, "Remember, you can do anything you want to if you wanna do it bad enough!" With an ear-to-ear grin he slapped my leg and shouted, "Let's go!" Climbing into the front seat, he slammed the door shut.

Tricycle-gear planes are guided with a steering wheel, but Dad liked the old-fashioned ones—"tail draggers"—controlled with a stick. Dad called nosewheel planes "dogs" and the pilots who flew them "robot drivers." Admittedly, it's no easy task to guide a tail-dragger plane when it's on the ground, but he lacked no confidence that I could master the art.

"Add throttle," instructed Dad.

I pushed the black knob forward, and the engine roared louder and the plane bumped into motion.

"Left rudder."

With my foot I depressed the left pedal and the plane turned a little.

"Now straighten 'er out, right down the runway."

Watching out the side windows and concentrating with all my might, I tried to combine rudder and throttle to keep the plane aiming straight ahead. Without contest, taxiing constituted the most challenging part of flying.

We bumped along at a good clip down the strip, far from the airport where the grass ended in forest. "Now, hard right rudder and give 'er throttle," he called.

The plane's tail swung around in a one-eighty, and we were facing back the way we'd come.

"Good. Now, engine check."

Engine check meant I must rev the engine while holding the brakes. The plane remained stationary while the engine screamed for a brief moment.

"Cleared for takeoff!" shouted Dad. "Pour the coal to 'er!" Now the head rush! Releasing the brakes, I pushed the throttle steadily forward and the plane bumped and bounced down the runway.

"Stick forward!"

Between my knees, a black stick with a ball on top protruded up from the floor like the gearshift of a truck. I pushed it forward. Though I couldn't see the result, I knew that made the tail of the plane go up in the air—the first stage of liftoff.

The plane vibrated, hurtling faster and faster, trees and brush on either side degenerating into a green blur. To keep it straight I pushed one rudder or the other.

Over the din of the engine, Dad shouted, "Pull 'er up!"

I eased back on the stick and the plane nosed upward. We were airborne! Out the front cockpit window I could see only gray-blue and clouds. As trees and houses shrank below and the world expanded, intense concentration gave way to the unspeakable thrill of utter freedom.

"Level off."

I eased the stick forward while pulling the throttle back a little. The roar of the engine subsided.

Once in the air, flying is easy. Dad taught me to push the stick left or right, forward or back, to turn or go up or down. We also did intentional stalls. Pilots crash when they stall out for lack of having learned the appropriate response. To initiate a stall Dad had me pull the throttle way back and keep the nose up. The plane shook and shuddered. Then it flipped to one side and began to spin in a nosedive. Dad taught me how to stop this downward spiral by holding both rudder pedals and easing back on the stick. This enabled the plane to straighten out and recover.

Landing was tricky. The plane dropped down and down and the treetops rose up so close I thought for sure the wheels would catch in them as we approached the runway. Dad kept saying, "Pull back on the stick, back on the stick." The tail had to stay down so the plane touched the ground with the main gear just seconds before the tail wheel made contact. If the tail was too high, we could nose over and crash.

After my landings became proficient, he taught me his favorite trick, the side-slip. A strategic move by which Dad could set a plane down in half the distance required by most pilots, the side-slip required a certain combination of rudder and stick.

Before long I could taxi, take off, fly and land while Dad sat cross-armed and silent with a satisfied smirk of pride in his pilot daughter. It was exhilarating! On clear days we could look across the horizon and see Mount Saint Helens belching smoke. After flying for a while, we looked down and saw the school bus coming. Then we landed and Dad drove me to the bus.

Soon the other guys at the airport learned of the nine-year-old wench who could fly a plane. They told Dad, "There's no way that little girl lands the plane entirely herself! We know you're helping her."

"Well, haul yourselves out here tomorrow mornin' an' watch," Dad challenged. The following morning we had an audience lining the runway. Dad kept his hands up on the braces above the cockpit windshield while I landed the plane so the men watching could see he wasn't helping me. Had I soloed I would have set a new record as the youngest pilot.

In quiet moments Dad could be caught sketching odd-looking drawings of a bird with a man's head—the call of Mystery summoning him to his destiny. He dreamed of building an ornithopter—a man-powered aircraft that gains altitude by means of its wings flapping akin to those of a bird. No one had ever succeeded in creating such a machine, especially not one capable of flying high, above the "cushion" or "ground effect." Dad intended to build a flapping-wing aircraft powered by the pilot pumping a hydraulic mechanism. Weighing a mere 96 pounds, the wing would be strapped to the pilot's back. Takeoff would be accomplished by the pilot running a few steps, again in imitation of certain large birds.

Dad's dream had begun to emerge from the drawings. In the old barn a skeletal "flapping wing" took shape. After teaching flying in the mornings, he devoted remaining daylight to working on his invention. When finished, his marketing plan consisted of a gravity-defying flight across the Grand Canyon. It was a do-or-die commitment. If he reached the other side, he would have proven to the world that he had built the first-ever fully man-powered aircraft—a breakthrough for aviation. If the ornithopter failed, he would meet his death on the rocks below.

The following spring "Uccello" was finished. Mom and I helped paint the finished ornithopter in glinting white with red lettering. Crafted from featherlight high-tensile titanium, levers below its midpoint controlled hydraulic joints, allowing the wings to flap in a nearly imperceptible figure-eight motion mimicking that of a bird. On two occasions I arrived home from school to learn Dad had test-flown the wing. These perilous ventures aloft were intentionally performed in my absence.

Mystery Banished

Meanwhile the saga of The Dream rolled on. Nightly, before I drifted off to sleep, it swept me away for an hour or more, my treasured second life replete with holy romance and high adventure. The Team continued to rescue abducted citizens. Yet the lurking mystery of that hidden part of the lovely man cast a shadow of foreboding across our relationship. His increasing and unexplained retreats into solitude, and my inability to comfort or relieve his apparent distress, caused me deep heartache. His oft-repeated statement, "I have to break the power of the darkness," haunted me.

Then one dreadful, excruciating night, The Dream metamorphosed into a horror story. The lovely man was brutally tortured, his flesh torn to rags. Then, though immortal, he died. The paradise was desecrated and the two native horse-like creatures who had battled faithfully at our side throughout the years were bound in chains.

This lasted for only a few episodes, throughout which I wailed in agony and utter despair.

Then, as abruptly as it had spiraled into a nightmare, The Dream reversed once more. The man lived again, all glorious, radiant as the sun.

The man's apparent defeat and destruction had wrought victory. His suffering and restoration to life had "broken the power of the darkness." The enemies had been stripped of their power and could no longer abduct our citizens. The once-ragged captives now danced in joy and liberty. Peace had been won and freedom would reign forever.

But what a bizarre triumph! I could not fathom it. How had good arisen from such appalling calamity? Most puzzling of all . . . why did the man have to suffer so terribly to bring it to pass?

The mystery of The Dream both captivated and disconcerted me. Days stretched into weeks as I obsessed over it and grappled desperately to explain the strange, costly victory.

Why did the man have to suffer and die? How has his tragic death wrought life and liberty for the entire cosmos?

When that answer was not forthcoming, I resolved to do without it, but the answer to another question I could not forgo:

Is the man real? Does he exist?

That which throughout these months and years had manifested as a quiet wooing filtering into my soul through occasional stimuli, was now a deep, captivating and utterly unfathomable anomaly. The intensity of the mystery had multiplied. The tiny whisper now roared and the roar demanded explanation. I could not go on without knowing.

Was The Dream true? Was it real? Surely the lovely man existed. I could not live if he did not exist!

Two possible explanations churned in my brain. Perhaps the man was a figment of a foolish child's daydream, the outcome of an imagination so wild as to create that which did not have any being. Opposing this idea was the fact that The Dream hadn't arisen from my mind. The argument *But it wasn't from me. It just happened* kept repeating. Nevertheless, I held on to the "wild imagination" as an option. If my own mind had concocted the entire story, then the man did not exist.

The second explanation? He existed! If he existed, then he embodied a treasure of incalculable worth unmatched across the aeons of history. If he existed, then he and the holy love he epitomized merited nothing short of worship, and the mystery he embodied was no doubt that for which I wished to spend the rest of my life. A raging inferno within yearned to hurl my life at his feet in joyous abandon if only to live out my days in his beauteous company.

Holy. The word haunted me. Nothing I had ever encountered in life measured up to the lofty heights and fearsome depths of that word. Only in The Dream had I brushed shoulders with that which rose to such a stature of awe. The man was holy. Beyond human, beyond the earth, hailing from another realm. If the man existed, I had arrived at the threshold of mining a treasure surpassing the value of the world's gold and a glory rendering dull the brightest sun and star in the cosmos.

Is the man real? Does he exist? The lovely man must surely be real! The Dream must be true. The cry to know the answer tormented me throughout my days until the nights when my head touched my pillow.

There in the darkness I waited. The portal! Surely the portal would reveal it. Transiting into my other life, I would enter a fresh episode and so unlock the secret. In The Dream's continuation, understanding would dawn, revelation dispelling the nebulous shroud, the rune disclosed and laid bare.

But that night when I lay down on my bed, I slept and woke to find . . . I had not entered The Dream. Nor ever since. Not one more episode played behind my eyelids. The portal had closed. The Dream had ended. I could no longer soar with eagles. Mundane earthly me projected no more into the feisty warrior Talwyn. I was once again only Leanna.

The mystery of the lovely man would not be revealed.

One dark and sickening day, I decided I had waited long enough, fooled myself long enough. The Dream was not real and never would be. There was no great adventure, no dark worlds and evil abductors and no captives to rescue.

Most devastating of all, I concluded that the man, whom I had come to love more than life itself, was a figment of my foolhardy child's imagination. No man would ever love me with the purity of the man in The Dream. Reality had not in the history of the universe given rise to a hero who would undergo what he did to set others free. No one had ever "broken the power of the darkness." He was nothing but an illusion. Nobody like him existed. The intensity of love, passion and awe I had enjoyed in his presence could not possibly be mine in reality.

Why had I experienced his beauteous visage, only for him to be ripped away from me? Must my heart forever lie desecrated and bleeding, hewn in two by a hacksaw, flayed like a miserable carcass?

After exhausting every conceivable option, I at last resolved that I must forget The Dream entirely. I must not permit myself to be victimized by remorse. I would leave it behind and go on with life.

So with heavy heart I leveled all my mental guns against the memory of The Dream. I banished it from my thoughts, expelled it from my emotions and drove it from my soul. So complete was my assault on The Dream that soon I could no longer recall a single episode. With the contempt of a disenchanted lover I gratefully dug its grave deep, covered it with mortar and scoured away its memory from the surface down to the minute cracks and crevices of my life. Within a year I forgot there ever had been an experience called The Dream.

When I evicted The Dream from my life, I also slammed the door on Mystery. The world I concluded to be purely physical. Mundane matter might not be especially glorious, but at least it wasn't a fairy tale. What registered on my retinas could be touched with my hands and therefore could be depended upon to exist. The box of agates, once so cherished as microcosms of treasure hidden in darkness, I shoved under my bed forgotten and disgraced. No treasures lay hidden in darkness. My musings had proven fake. Neither magic nor the supernatural had any being in reality. Nothing was holy. There was no mystery and no particular destiny called to me. No secret beckoned from beyond the treetops, and my interpretation of the whip-poor-will's voice epitomized stupid childhood fantasies. Now I knew better. What became of my life depended upon me. I would create my own future by means of my wits, my hard work, my ability to assert myself and my adeptness at kicking aside anybody who barred my way.

My parents' near-annual routine—move to a new climate, pay cash for a chunk of land out in the boonies and build a house before winter—wasn't going to work in Washington. The dense population offered no boonies by our standards and Dad's daily griping, "There's a house behind every tree," accentuated the drear of the perpetual drizzle. The cost of a parcel of land exceeded that which my parents had saved up. Debt being in their mind equivalent to slavery, they concluded we couldn't afford to stay in Washington.

"Uccello" served as the final instigator of our fifth trek across the western two-thirds of the United States. Health issues had so far prevented Dad from challenging the Grand Canyon. While recovering, he endeavored to at least display the crowning glory of his lifetime of aeronautical discovery at the aircraft extravaganza held annually in Oshkosh, Wisconsin.

As usual the Cinquanta family included us three, two ponies and one collie dog. To haul the ponies we acquired a rickety wooden trailer that threatened to fall apart with every bump in the road. At an auction we procured a second car—a Dodge Swinger—for $500. Starting it involved a three-step process: After turning the key, Dad flipped a switch under the dashboard and then twisted together two wires hanging down from another part of the dashboard. With a spark and an electrical "*snap!*" the starter reluctantly turned over and the engine—usually—roared to life. We never bothered to remove the keys because the ignition contraption would have befuddled an expert thief.

Ponies in the trailer behind the old blue Dodge Dart and Dad's dismantled airplane strapped on top of the Swinger pulling the camper trailer, like a caravan of classic hippies from the sixties, we set off across the mountains heading east. Mom sang, "Yellow Rose of Texas" or "Mockingbird Hill" and munched homemade snacks to keep herself awake. When Dad felt sleepy he ate dates. Dad led because Mom had a way of getting her left and right mixed up. To signal a potty break Mom switched her headlights on and Dad pulled over. Before dusk we parked at a KOA campground. We let the ponies out of the trailer and tied them with long ropes so they could enjoy some grass. Mom prepared the standard meal of fried potatoes and chicken and vegetables in our twelve-foot house-on-wheels.

I had come to love the open highway with its ever-changing landscape, the shadow of the car and trailer rippling against the weeds in the ditch, the wind whipping my hair and the constant intrigue of what lay around the next bend. Sticking my brown arm out the window, I surfed the wind or imagined I was galloping a powerful horse in the field alongside the car negotiating ditches, weaving through forests and laughingly soaring over formidable obstacles. On hot afternoons the heat waves rising from the pavement conveyed illusions of a watery paradise ahead, a mysterious land of adventure. We drove and drove, but the shimmery horizon kept moving, staying barely out of reach, evading the grasp of my hand, beyond the physical, waking, real-world life. It was one of those ruminative moments when Mystery would have come calling, beckoning, saying, *There's more . . . beyond the horizon. . . .*

But now I saw only a mirage, heat waves on pavement, a scientifically explainable atmospheric phenomenon. Mystery's banishment would not be recalled. It had deceived me, and I vowed never again to grant it access to my life.

The Bat House

Full circle back in Wisconsin, a friend permitted us to camp our caravan on his back forty.

Gusts of encroaching winter blew brown leaves into our twelve-foot camper. We'd have to move into a real house before snow flew. By looking in the newspaper for country places to rent, Mom discovered an old farm, complete with a house and a cow barn for the ponies. It bordered a field and was surrounded by trails and lakes, the promise of plenteous riding fun for Mom and me. The house had fallen into disrepair, with siding peeling off and plaster crumbling, but none of that mattered to us. The houses we built rarely reached the stage of plaster or siding anyway. Best of all, as far as my parents were concerned, the rent was only $100 a month. Elated, we moved in.

Everything that's too good to be true usually is, and we promptly discovered the reason for the low rent. The walls of the house had been invaded by bats! In the evening, streams of the eerie creatures poured out from chinks under the eaves. Add a ghost in the window and a scraggy tree on a moonlit night, and it could be argued we lived in a classic haunted house.

The coming and going of the bats would not have been particularly troublesome excepting that on occasion one found its way into the house. A hidden gap in the wall of my bedroom provided their port of entry. On such nights I wakened to *whoosh* . . . *whoosh* and an attesting breeze as bat wings stirred the darkness overhead.

My fondness of fuzzy, warty and slimy critters did not include bats. The first time I saw one up close and personal, I got the heebie-jeebies. Their claws and webbed wings aren't scary compared to their heads. They have a gruesome face akin to a gargoyle, with a gaping mouth and vicious little fangs, and their beady black eyes snarl, *Give me one chance to savor your blood!*

At the sound of bat wings in the air, I impulsively yanked the blanket over my head and hollered, *"Dad! Bat!"* My parents dashed into my room and flicked on the light.

"Keep your head covered or it'll get in your hair," ordered Dad. The temptation to participate in the bat chase was enormous, but the thought of a live bat entangled in my long brown hair elicited the unusual response of unquestioning obedience. I stayed in bed, peering out while keeping the sheet pulled tightly over my hair.

Mom grabbed the butterfly net and Dad a towel, weapons kept handy for the explicit purpose of whomping bats. Then the hunt began.

"It's up there, on the curtain rod." Mom pointed. Dad moved in with the towel. *Whomp!* Missed. The bat flew around, and Mom lit out after it with the butterfly net. *Swat!* Missed.

Dad stalked about the room, towel poised. "You see where it's hiding?"

"There!" Spying the black body wedged between the rafter and the ceiling, I stuck a hand out long enough to point.

Whomp!

The bat flew around again and then hurtled down the stairwell with Mom and Dad in hot pursuit. Eventually the hunters prevailed; the bat was whomped and chucked out the door and everyone returned to bed.

Whenever we happened to be living in a real house, I situated my bed directly beneath an open window, because I loved the sounds of the night and the cool breeze. But at the bat house the night sounds were not so pleasant. I dozed off serenaded by the creepy sound of two or three bats clinging to the outside of the screen, scratching and ruffling and trying to squeeze inside.

The odor was far worse than the bats themselves. The bats lived in the upper part of the walls, and their urine and feces seeped through, decorating the wallpaper with brown blotches. In the summer I slept downstairs to escape the toxic stench.

I was now thirteen, and my insatiable equestrian zeal necessitated a real horse instead of a pony. My folks scraped and scrounged and collected $4,000, but the European Warmbloods over which I drooled came with price tags upward of

$25,000. Thus dwindled my hopes of owning one of those powerful floating equine wonders. Then one day we happened upon an ad for a green-broke European Warmblood filly. She had injured herself at the age of two and now bore an unsightly hump over her loin called a "roach back." Her price had been marked down to—$4,000! We dug the half-rotten horse trailer out of the snowbank and drove one thousand miles to Denver to buy my dream horse.

Alpenglow and I had our falling-outs, but gradually we progressed in the discipline of dressage. Soon I expressed my intention to compete, but one problem rendered my desire nigh impossible. Over a hundred miles separated our home from the nearest dressage shows, and an enormous 1,250-pound Alpen could barely be stuffed into the rickety trailer that moreover faced impending disintegration. We possessed no means by which to purchase a trailer and no budget for motel rooms or restaurant food. But lack of money had no power to thwart my enterprising parents from giving me whatever I set my heart on. Perpetual inventors, they remedied both problems by designing a horse trailer that doubled as motel and kitchen. Dad purchased two axles and built the trailer/motel from scratch. After the horses were out, the inner panels folded down into a comfortable bed complete with four-inch mattresses. The front area included a cookstove and dressing room. Innovative and practical beyond all the factory-made trailers on the showgrounds, Dad enjoyed exhibiting his invention to curious gawkers while my horse and I battled for ribbons.

Usually on the way home from the show in the hot afternoon, the old $500 Dodge Swinger either overheated or the alternator broke or a tire blew out or the fan went kaput. Dad hitched a ride to the nearest gas station for water to dump in and over the radiator, or to an auto shop to buy parts. Mom and I sat by the rig doling out nibbles of hay to an impatient Alpen and shuddered each time a semi careened past, a few feet away from creaming us.

If any kid on the planet had enjoyed the benefits of a privileged, love-smothered, joy-filled childhood it was me, but despite it all, my life grew darker. From the time I banished Mystery and evicted The Dream, my moral fortitude spiraled downward and I became the categorical opposite of the noble beauty I had once revered and cherished. I refused to do chores, lost my temper over trivialities and once even dared take a swing at Mom when she attempted to discipline me for mouthing off in front of a guest. Some might call it "teenage rebellion syndrome," but I had no reasonable excuse for my putrefying turdship. Corrupt, villainous thoughts swirled about in my brain like poop in a stuck toilet. Naughty words, mean reactions, selfish motives and an arrogant "I'm cooler than you, get the h*** out of my way" attitude rendered me a bona fide pain in the bumpkin.

But Mystery, once invested and embraced, will not forever tolerate deposition. My smug, self-gratifying material-only world was about to be flipped on its head.

2

The Encounter

A romp upon the mountains brilliant nature
  shining bright
But all the vista's splendor and creation's
  grand delight
Dim and dull is rendered in the face of
  Love's true light

Not that love for self or fame, not of earth
  or man
Not which waits for deeds of might nor
  scorns the feeble hand
Love awaits to lavish grace and bleeds to
  ransom life and land.

Different Kind of Love

*D*ave Cutsforth was a jolly bloke whom Dad had taught
to fly years ago. Each year Dave took the time to find

out on what remote piece of geography the Cinquantas had staked a claim. Then whenever his business travels brought him within two hundred miles of us he'd get a rental car and traipse out to pay us a visit.

Near their home in Grand Rapids, Minnesota, the Cuts-forths had built a private airport and hangar with attached apartment. Ever since leaving the first Hawks Haven in the Wisconsin woods, Dad lacked a hangar in which to work on airplanes, so for years Dave had encouraged us to come live in the apartment and build airplanes in the hangar. Equipped with central heating and a concrete floor, the facility ranked five star by our standards. Stubborn independence had inspired my parents to resist the offer for ten years, but at last they decided to accept. In exchange for the use of his facility, Dave only asked that Dad modify his airplane and teach his sons to fly.

The idea of moving to Grand Rapids filled me with excitement for multiple enterprising reasons. The long grassy runway offered an excellent place to train my horses. A cliff looming above one portion of the runway dared me to conquer it. And last but not least, Dave's nephew Curt was my age and unbearably cute.

Grand Rapids lay a few hundred miles northwest of our residence, so instead of renting a U-Haul as in most other moves, Dave with his Suburban and trailer helped us relocate. I found myself strangely attracted to Dave. He evoked an aura of the divine, an otherworldly presence. Once while he drove a trailer load of our possessions to Grand Rapids, I dared to ride with him. I sensed myself to be in the presence of royalty, but at the same time I felt ashamed to entertain such foolish thoughts. Anybody could see he was just a man, and an adult besides.

Neither of us uttered a word, but while we drove along he played a cassette in the tape deck. The chorus of one tune further confirmed my wonderment and emblazoned itself on my memory:

> Walking into the enemy's camp, laying our weapons down,
> shedding our armor as we go and leaving it on the ground . . .[1]

The lyric made no sense. It confounded reason. Nobody lays their weapons down when approaching an enemy! Ludicrous! The conundrum demanded elucidation but shyness forbade me from inquiring about its meaning. Throughout the journey to Grand Rapids and for weeks afterward, I stewed in my curiosity. Ever so gently Mystery once again tapped at my closed door.

Mom began frequenting the church attended by Dave's family, and one day she towed me along. When the first kid I bumped into was Curt, I knew we could turn church into a revelrous blowout.

The other female youngsters who attended the church disdained my ecclesiastical naïveté and distanced themselves from me. Their prissy "we're holier than thou" attitude evoked in me the sensation of nausea and so we avoided one another like the plague.

But I was not the lone misfit.

Mandy reeked of cigarettes and wore dark leather clothes and spikes. A steel ring pierced her eyebrow and lip and three hung from each ear. She freely employed a generous

1. Jerry Williams, "The Army of the Lord," Acappella, *Conquerors*, 1986. Used by permission of The Acappella Company.

vocabulary of forbidden words. If I had grown up "woods" and "barn," she had grown up "street," traveling the carnal paths from which my parents had so carefully shielded me. Despite our stark dissimilarities she and I hit it off on account of one essential commonality: naughtiness.

Mandy and Curt and I knew we didn't belong in church. Our mothers had dragged us there against our will. Making the best of our unhappy dilemma, we determined to extract as many laughs as we could drum up.

Sunday school commenced and we trooped into the room. In the middle of a semicircle of chairs stood an easel and marker board. Phil, the youth leader, opened with prayer, scratched a Bible passage on the board and proceeded to tell us a story about an old man and a boat.

Within five minutes boredom weighed upon my eyelids. Curt and Mandy on my left and right drooped likewise. Phil's voice faded as we began to whisper, poke each other and pass messages.

"Curt!"

The ruddy youth snapped to wide-eyed attention.

"Please tell us the name of the man in the story."

Curt froze. His gaping mouth could produce not a word in reply. Muffled snickers rippled through the group. Phil shot Curt a stern look and pointed to an empty chair on the other side of the semicircle.

Smirking askance, he strutted over and plopped into the assigned seat. Mandy made faces at him and mouthed, "Way to go, dude!"

Class proceeded.

After long minutes of strained attention, I raised my hand.

"Yes, Leanna?"

"May I be excused to go to the bathroom?"

"Yes, you may." Phil returned to his marker board.

A brilliant idea had burst into my head having nothing to do with relieving myself. Once beyond the classroom door I swiftly noted the coast was clear. Muffled vibes of the pastor's sermon wafted through closed sanctuary doors. I darted down the stairs, wary in case I should encounter a human around the bend. In another classroom children chattered and laughed. The little farts were having fun. Not quite as much as I would be a few moments from now.

Four strides carried me into the kitchen. A brief rummage in the drawers and I had procured the munitions—a few drinking straws. Back upstairs in the bathroom I stuffed toilet paper in my pockets and made my reappearance to class in the three minutes required to have genuinely taken a piss.

Passing Curt on my way back to my seat I slipped him a straw and a wad, to which he squelched a whoop and exchanged an inconspicuous low-five. Trembling with glee I sat down and put on an innocent face. When Phil wasn't looking I armed Mandy likewise. Then the fun began. When Phil turned away from us to write on the marker board, spit wads flew. The rest of the boys struggled in vain to muffle snickers while the other girls, proper and behaved as princesses, shot dagger eyes at us.

Phil stopped and looked hard at us. "Leanna! Mandy! What's that in your hands?"

Giggles.

"Please put those straws down."

We obliged by placing our plastic bazookas on the edges of our chairs.

"No, on the floor."

Onto the floor went the straws.

A few minutes of order ensued before we retrieved our weapons. Splat! A spit wad hit the marker board, narrowly missing Phil's head. This time he continued teaching hoping in the absence of response his tormentors might desist. The rest of the hour amalgamated complete distraction facilitated by myself, Curt and Mandy, intercepted by attempted restoration of order by Phil and the handful of mannered girls who indicated their vexation toward us with rolling eyes and incensed gestures.

Too soon class ended and it was time to split. I made a beeline for the door, but too late. . . . Phil was in front of me. I wished desperately I could transform into a beetle and crawl under the carpet or vanish into the air. Neither option presented itself. *Oh well,* I consoled myself. *Whatever chastisement he pronounces upon me is well-deserved.*

Then the unexpected happened; he put his arm around my shoulders and gave me a squeeze. Heat surged through me, a combination of abashment and confusion.

He had positioned himself beside and not in front of me, for which I was grateful, because it saved me from having to look in his face. From the corner of my eye I could detect he was smiling. "Leanna, I'm praying for you." His voice was quiet and contained not a trace of anger.

My lips muttered a generic "Okay," but with indignant defiance rebellion silently snarled, *Yeah right, I don't need prayer!* My brain queried, *Why the heck does he care a hoot about me? I deliberately made a mess of his class.*

Week after week along with the rowdy boys, I did my best to disrupt class and make mischief. An unspoken goal served as my motivation. I endeavored to drive Phil so insane with frustration he'd desist from praying for me and do the logical—throw me out or at least harshly reprimand me in front of the boys. Thus I aspired to win the prize of chief deviant.

However to my continued bewilderment, Sunday after Sunday Phil kept on showing me uncanny kindness. This man exemplified a mysterious divergence from the norm. The aura I had sensed around Dave exuded from him as well. He existed in a higher realm.

I figured myself to be a Christian. After all, I certainly wasn't a Buddhist or Hindu or Muslim. My heritage as bred-and-born American I supposed made me a Christian. But I did not believe in God, much less Jesus. God was far too ethereal. Whatever existed had skin or hide or bark that I could touch and see and smell. My skin and ears discerned the wind and my emotions sensed anger and love. But God could neither be seen, heard nor felt, so according to me, He didn't exist.

Nevertheless, I mused, wouldn't life explode with magnificence if my observations were wrong? What a grand wonderland of adventure may swing open to a human soul if the world extended beyond the realm of the physical!

An essence long dormant stirred. Ignited once again by the light that shone from within these two humble, powerful men, the cry sang again through my soul—the call of the whip-poor-will, the call of Mystery.

This arousal didn't qualify as an all-consuming thirst, nor even a daily thought. It flitted into my cognizance and out again, like the little birds hovering momentarily to peck the suet dangling from a tree limb outside our kitchen window. But whenever Mystery stirred, unconsciously I found myself thinking, *God, I don't believe in You. But in case You do exist, please show Yourself to me.*

He did.

Steel versus Angel

In Minnesota options for synthesizing snow into fun abounded especially on Saturdays. The weekly ritual found Curt and me and motley friends firing up our snowmobiles and tearing up and down the runway over drifts and mounds and through woodsy trails. Tiring of that, we hitched the twelve-foot toboggan to Dave's 150 HP Arctic Cat and competed to see who could stay on the longest. I had mastered "kamikaze" position—the whiplashing tail end of the sled. I prided myself further in managing to stay on while riding backward, ice crystals kicked up by the end of the sled stinging my face as I crouched precariously on my knees with mittens locked into the ropes like a bull rider.

Lunch warming my tummy, the last "good-bye" of the last friend signaled time to take a drive to Sugar Lodge Resort and go skiing. Dad had taught me to drive at the age of eight. Now barely fifteen, my permitted range of solo motoring extended no farther than the one-mile stretch of rural blacktop from Dave's place to the ski mountain—which accorded my ski trips dual motives.

Modern ski bindings can be released easily by stepping down on a little plastic release with the opposite foot, but my skis—hand-me-downs outgrown by Dave's kids—featured old-fashioned bindings. Releasing them involved jamming a ski pole into a steel tube at the heel and prying upward.

Three whole days passed in which I managed not to wipe out a single time, and I had made it through six days without colliding with another skier. Thus I concluded myself master of the art and smarter than my teachers. Dave had counseled me to keep my bindings loose so when I crashed, the skis would come off instead of twisting my leg into a pretzel. But three reasons fueled my noncompliance: Since early childhood I had been engaged in a perpetual search for schemes by which to evade anything that smelled of an order—even an order from Dave. Second, after taking a tumble I dreaded the conspicuous trudge up the hill to retrieve my skis. For those few embarrassing moments I was certain every skier on the slope and even the trees were laughing at me. Third, I interpreted the act of keeping my bindings loose as an admission of incompetence.

So one day behind closed doors I took a screwdriver and cranked those bindings until they were so tight the ski pole bent when I pried them off.

In accordance with my invasion-hungry temperament, I studied a map of the ski runs and proposed to "conquer" them by skiing down each at least once without crashing. This feat I had all but accomplished. Even the formidable Thunders—the black diamond slopes—had been subdued beneath my flying runners, I having managed to schuss each at least once without biting the snow.

A single solitary slope remained undefeated, the reason being, I couldn't find it. The map showed its location in the middle of a long cross-country stretch through the woods between the beginner/intermediate hills and the Thunders. I had skied past the spot countless times but the alleged slope eluded my view. The unsolved mystery tormented me. I vowed that if ever the hidden monster be discovered, no matter how steep, I would conquer it!

One frigid day Mystery invaded my smug egotistical cavorts in a most chilling brush with death.

Mom, who readily acknowledged her novicehood, had accompanied me to the ski resort prepared to frequent the Bunny Hill. The tow rope and gentle slope were, I perceived, fit only for little farts, old fogies, beginners and the faint of heart. Between us we possessed a single set of poles. Pride ballooning my ego, I handed the poles to Mom. "These dumb sticks are a nuisance, you take 'em." With that I set off toward Thunders. My primary but undisclosed goal was to locate the elusive hill and conquer it.

This time upon approaching the spot, I noticed a little rise in the terrain and an apparent clearing in the trees beyond. Breathless, I sidestepped up to it. Sure enough, dropping away on the other side descended the slope! But now I saw the run was no longer in use. Dense brush had grown up and stood four feet above the deep, ungroomed snow. The lift had fallen into disrepair and was not operating.

But I was undeterred. One thought seethed within: I had to conquer the final slope and fulfill my self-proclaimed dare. So with no further ado, I launched over the edge.

My skis immediately disappeared in the soft snow and I could neither snowplow nor christie. Powder-skiing far exceeded my skill level. I found myself hurtling straight down and rapidly accelerating. Brush smacked me in the face and tore at my body. Still, I estimated that if the incline didn't steepen I could make it to the bottom.

At that instant the slope dropped off to a near cliff! Instinctive self-preservation at last overriding my insanity, I realized if I didn't stop now I might kill myself. Throwing my body sideways I shoulder-rolled, accumulating my share of scuffs and pokes while plummeting through brush and prickles. By the time gravity and momentum were exhausted, I embodied the abominable snowman. Frozen crystals were ground into my clothes and packed up my pant legs and down my neck and up my sleeves.

Nevertheless, with profound satisfaction I announced to myself, "Adventure complete!" At least I had found the hill, attacked it and given it a good run for its money.

After brushing off the top layer of snow and digging as much as possible out of my apparel, I assessed the available routes back to civilization. Below and to both sides of the hill stretched dense, trackless forest. To return the way I'd come proved my singular option. *No sweat*, I thought. *I'll take off my skis and walk up the hill.*

Possessing no tool with which to pry, I broke off the sturdy-looking trunk of one of the bushes. Ripping off the branches and breaking it to a three-foot length, I stuck it in the metal tube protruding from the back of my ski boot, and pried. The pliable green pole bent. I broke it in half and tried again. It bent into a miserable arc. The ski boot binding didn't budge.

The deep snow concealed the dry sticks and larger pieces of wood that might have otherwise been available. I managed to procure a sturdy-looking dry tree branch and jammed the end into the metal tube. Hoping against hope, I pulled. *Crack!* It broke.

Fear began to come over me. I decided to try with my hands. Risking the loss of precious warmth, I sat down and pulled off my mittens. Grasping the frigid metal, I strained with all my might. I might as well have been an ant presuming to bend an iron rod. The task proved so futile I felt foolish even trying. The binding remained locked down on my boot.

I sat still for a moment. Under other conditions I would have welcomed being out in the woods alone. Nature was my friend. But now the lonesomeness of the deep forest where not a human soul was to be found brought with it a terrifying realization. I was trapped. A casualty of my own foolhardiness and lust for adventure. I had parlayed myself into a spot where even the ski patrol wouldn't look for me if Mom reported me missing. Icy claws gripped my soul upon realization that . . . I was face-to-face with the possibility of freezing to death.

One option remained. I could climb back up the hill with my skis on. Lifting one ski at a time I tried to sidestep up the hill. On hard-packed snow and in the absence of obstacles, this isn't particularly difficult. But now sidestepping soon proved impossible due to the dense brush and soft, deep snow. My long, clumsy skis hooked in the brush at each attempt to take a step, causing me to fall. Falling again and again, my desperation escalated and I struggled harder. Mired deeper and deeper in the snow, I grew exhausted, and with fatigue I grew cold. The afternoon sun threatened to sink behind the hill, and an extra-chill wind whipped across the bleak hillside.

Until that day on the ski mountain I had not once in my life genuinely uttered a prayer. The Lord's Prayer Mom taught me to recite at the breakfast table amounted to little more than a parent-imposed ritual before digging in to eggs or pancakes. I had determined that God didn't exist, and until today I deemed myself to have done well without Him.

But now my enterprising wit in which I'd trusted had failed. There was no way out. I was in a real mess. Minutes ticked by. Again and again I strained at the bindings with my hands and began to tremble with a mixture of fear and cold.

At last, self-conscious despite the obvious lack of observers, I muttered a mental prayer. *Uh . . . God, if You're there, please help me.*

The moment I cast this prayer into the heavens, something was set into motion. The waning rays of sun grew overwhelmingly bright. Warmth flooded my body from head to foot. With arc lamp intensity the snow, the forest, the sky swelled with such glaring radiance I had to squint. At the same time I was enveloped in an unexplainable peace as if cuddled up on the sofa at home wrapped in a mink-soft blanket.

Before I could wonder what was happening, my right hand was removing the mitten from my left. Then my left hand reached involuntarily for my left ski binding. I thought, *Why am I doing this? I already tried five times. This is stupid.* But guided by an unseen force, my hand continued on its course. My fingers touched the cold steel.

Then something happened that completely defies reason; the ski binding opened. The ski fell off my boot!

I stared dumbfounded. I hadn't strained, hadn't even properly wrapped my fingers around the metal tube. Yet there lay my ski in the snow. My boot was free!

Before my brain could stop reeling, my right hand reached to the right binding. The ski fell off the moment my fingers touched it.

I sat there stunned. What had happened? I had spent the last hour struggling and straining and now my skis were off with no effort whatsoever.

In complete shock, I picked up my skis and walked up the hill. My pride at having found and challenged the rogue hill was obliterated. My mind groped and clawed to make sense of what had transpired. This bizarre occurrence had to be explained with a rational answer.

"I'm going to ski back to the lodge," I pronounced, "and there I shall remove my skis again with my bare hands. I shall prove this was nothing but chance!"

Returning to the lodge, I sat down in the safety of civilization with hundreds of ski poles stuck in the snow, readily accessible. There I attempted to again remove my ski with my bare hands. No go. A mouse trying to bend a crowbar.

In my natural strength there was no way I could have taken those skis off. What happened up on that hill was unexplainable. That an extraterrestrial power had come to my aid and released my bindings remained the only "rational explanation" possible.

Mystery had broken in on me in broad daylight.

Nevertheless, like Pharaoh, I hardened my heart. I pushed the incident aside as a freak happening, chance or luck and went on my merry way.

Mystery is patient. It hopes we will heed its beckonings. When we don't, Mystery may with reckless determination employ unusual means to gain our attention. Invading our conceited little world, Mystery grabs us, transforms us in a moment and launches us forth in a completely different direction.

The mystery beyond the treetops—the one I had written off as a mere fantasy—now prepared to burst out of the misty shadows into stark reality. And it would do so in its most awesome, shocking and holy form.

Face-to-Face

A new year had begun—1986. March arrived, attended by melting snow and warmer breezes after six months of Minnesota deep freeze. Cocky as ever, I aimed to enjoy another summer of mischief and pushing limits. But my plans were about to be invaded.

The downstairs of our bi-level apartment behind the airplane shop consisted of kitchen, living room and Mom and Dad's bedroom. Upstairs were two rooms. Mom's sewing machine and my art materials occupied one. The other, situated nearest the stairwell, served as my bedroom. In my room a narrow walkway separated my bed from a cot where my friends slept when they stayed overnight.

The night of March 27 began like every other. After an uneventful day at school I had pitched my backpack on the couch, grabbed a cookie and made a beeline for the barn to ride my horse. After supper I burned through my homework then studied horsemanship books till bedtime.

Around five o'clock in the morning I awoke. Premature rays of light filtering through the window sufficed to reveal slightly more than shadows in the room. Teenagers love to sleep late, but the responsibility of feeding the horses had molded into me a habit of rising at 7 a.m. Nevertheless 5 a.m. was *too* early.

Turning over on my back, I stared indignantly at the ceiling. Sleep had departed for good. Two long hours of tossing and turning lay ahead. Prone to the typical teenaged negativism when life didn't cater to my wishes, I breathed a swear word and muttered, "This sucks. Why did I wake up so early?"

"THERE'S SOMEONE IN THE GUEST BED."

A voice had spoken out of the darkness! An audible voice! *"Who is in my room?"*

A man's voice? Oh my gosh! Someone had gotten into my room! Terror shrieked through my bones, immobilizing me, freezing my heart. No, I was not dreaming! A moment earlier I might have still been drowsy, but now I was fully and widely awake.

I flipped over onto my stomach, and my saucer-wide eyes strained into the blackness—the far corner of the room from whence the voice emanated. No figure. No movement. But it was so dark, anyone could be there. Anything. Would someone—or something—emerge from the shadows? I waited, fists knotted with the blankets, my heart not daring to beat.

When nothing moved or appeared, the words I had heard began to register. . . . The voice had informed me, "There's someone in the guest bed." Almost too frightened to look, I found my eyes turning toward the bed barely a foot removed from mine.

What I saw injected a shot of adrenaline. Before I could think, I was cowering back against the wall ready to scream.

There was a hump under the blankets!

My heart jackhammered in my throat. A thousand terrors tumbled over themselves as I realized again . . . *This is not a dream! This is real!* Questions swirled. *Who is in my room? How did a strange person sneak into our house? Did we forget to lock the door? What might this person do to me?*

The figure lay motionless, as if asleep. *What is it?* I thought. *Human? Not human?* I had on occasion watched a scary movie, and now visions of monsters crawling out from under people's beds rushed at me in dreadful imagery.

Raw terror sucked my skin corpselike and clammy. A scream pushed up into my throat, obliging release. I had to do something. I could not remain passively sitting here on this bed.

Eyes riveted on the mysterious sleeping figure, I began to creep over the front end of my bed toward the door of the room.

The bedsprings squeaked. I froze, eyes riveted on the hump in the guest bed.

No movement.

I placed one foot on the floor, then the other. Gingerly I stood. The floorboards creaked. I froze again, certain that whatever was in the bed would come roaring to life. Step by step I inched my way across the room to the light switch.

I stood there with my hand on the switch. If I turned the light on, the sleeper would awake. That possibility was too scary. I didn't turn on the light.

The logical action I suppose would have been to go downstairs and rouse my parents. Instead, after standing there for a long, tense moment, I found myself slinking back to my bed. Taking great care to make no sound, I climbed back over the front of the bed and pulled the covers up so I could pretend to be sleeping. There I cowered, waiting and watching.

The figure moved. Swallowing another urge to scream, I stayed still. He sat up on the side of the bed.

There my fear ended.

The person was Jesus!

Artists picture Jesus as a stately Caucasian blond or brunette, head and shoulders above the rabble, with blue eyes, a spotless white robe and a halo over His head.

That is not how I saw Him.

Being of Jewish descent, He was average in stature with black hair and olive skin. But I could not tell whether He was handsome or homely because of the state in which I saw Him.

Right before my eyes I saw Jesus in His time of suffering. His face was bloody and bruised and His eyes blackened from repeated beatings. Blood caked His hair and trickled from wounds on His head.

His clothes were tattered and blood-soaked. According to history, Jesus was beaten 39 times with a bone-laced whip. This instrument of torture had shredded not only the garment, but also His flesh.

With vehemence far eclipsing my former terror, now a revelation exploded through my being, igniting every sinew and synapse. Truth like an injection shot into my soul. Questions were obliterated and three grand and indisputable facts blazed neon-bright in my vision:

GOD EXISTS.
JESUS IS REAL.
THE BIBLE IS THE WORD OF GOD.

In that moment I knew that were I the only person in the world, He would have suffered this for me. He endured this for every person, no matter how good or bad. This knowledge exceeded a mental persuasion. A surgical implantation had been sutured into my soul, a laser operation straight from the supernatural realm.

Usually if you do wrong and hurt someone, the person is angry with you. But in the bruised and scarred face of Jesus, there was no condemnation, no anger, but pure forgiveness and compassion.

I could endure only a brief look in His face. My mind swooned. Every muscle felt like water. *I am . . . in the presence of God. God in the form of a man . . . and He has suffered terribly to purchase my freedom!* The reality of it swirled in my mind and my body went limp. I fell on my face on my bed, weeping. The intensity of that moment is unexplainable and beyond words. My tears arose not so much from anguish as from awe and reverence, the single possible response for a mortal when found in the presence of the Holy One. But they were also tears of grief that such divine beauty had to be so marred for my pardon.

Then something happened that drove the experience still deeper.

He touched me.

He reached out His hand and laid it on my right shoulder. "My child, don't cry." His voice was gentle but strong.

My arms trembled as they lifted my torso from the bed. *It's too much for me*, I thought. *I cannot look into His eyes again.* But I knew I must. Like magnets they drew me. He had more to show me, more to impart. In His countenance, so tortured and yet so selfless, I beheld a love that no human can imagine.

But enthroned upon that love, a still higher revelation now pierced my soul. His sufferings' accomplishment exceeded personal pardon. A victorious light shone from His battered face, an aura of triumph and glory, the persona of One who has conquered all and now reigns supreme. The suffering He had endured constituted the price to rescue the world. I was witnessing the battle scars necessary to break the power of evil.

In a communication superseding words, buoyed up with a joyous lilt like the song of angels, I heard Him declare, *I've broken the power of darkness. The citizens can be set free forever.* Then His love was flowing into me, washing over me, waves of splendor engulfing my soul.

Placing my left hand on His while it rested on my shoulder, I felt the hole, where His wrist had been nailed to the cross. *This is not a dream!* My mind swooned again with the repeating fact. *This is real. I am not asleep. This is real. I am face-to-face with God!*

Awe and reverence once more overcame me. I gazed upon the One who had suffered for our freedom, the One who conquered death. For love He had subjected Himself to this unfathomable suffering—love for me, to ransom my life. I gazed into the eyes of a being who embodied self-sacrificing beauty, a being for whom no word but one could suffice. . . . He was

. . . *holy*. The weight of it overpowered me. Unable to contain or bear up under the glory of His presence and the dreadfulness of His pain, I again fell facedown on my bed weeping.

Golden rays kissed my tousled locks. Daylight! As if ejected off my mattress, I found myself on my feet. Knees shaking, I stood between the two beds. The whole encounter rushed back before my eyes. Mottled bright spots of sun beaming through tree branches outside the window illumined the guest bed. It was neat and perfectly made. It bore no visible sign of the presence who had lain there a few hours earlier. But for me the bed was now sacred. I feared to touch it.

Something was different. Something had changed. For a long, strange moment I stood gawking about the room, not daring to move a muscle. Against the wall stood my dresser, deep chestnut-varnished oak with great round mirror above. There were my three Breyer horses, the only childhood treasures I had managed to confiscate the night we had picked up and left Arizona. My half-finished mural of a great black steed still leaped over the mirror and the paintbrushes lay atop a nearby stool, awaiting my next bout of artistic inspiration.

"I am alive." I dared to draw a tremorous breath. "And this is my room. I am on Planet Earth."

But I felt so other, so strange, like a worm that goes to sleep in its cocoon and wakes up a butterfly. Like my operating system had been rebuilt and reprogrammed.

With these thoughts another terror crept over me. Had I undergone a physical transformation? Had I become something or someone else? Images of Alice in Wonderland drifted into my mind, and I impulsively touched my body, examined my hands, my arms.

"Flesh. Alive. Me." I dared another breath.

But what about my face?

With terrified eyes I stared across the room at the mirror. A few paces would reveal the dread answer. My legs trembled. What would I see in the mirror? Had I metamorphosed into another person, or—creature?

Sick with fear I summoned enough courage to step in front of the mirror.

Whew! I still looked like me. But I didn't feel like me. I felt sparkly inside, a crystal vase from the dishwasher squeaky-clean.

I must have eaten breakfast because if I hadn't my parents would have inquired as to my manner of illness, but I could not tell whether I ate cereal or pancakes or eggs. During those few minutes downstairs I learned, to my further awe, that today was Good Friday. I had seen Him on the very day when followers of Jesus commemorate His death.

Throughout my uneasy time in the presence of normal humans, I kept checking my body and worrying. I felt like a light bulb, as if the brightness within was glowing through my skin. Surely others could see it. What if my parents exclaimed, "You look different!" What would I answer? If I had attempted to speak I would have stammered. The world reeled. I feared to walk, certain my steps would resemble a plastered wino.

I have to get away! my mind cried. *Let me find a place alone, secluded, and attempt to process this.*

Withdrawing to my room, I opened my paint cans, climbed on my stool and dabbled at the mural. Downstairs, Mom had the radio on, as was her habit while cooking. She usually played a Christian station, which I had trained myself to ignore. But now my paintbrush froze in midstroke when Petra's "The Coloring Song" wafted through the air and into my ears.

The lyrics vividly described how the blood had flowed down the face of Jesus, God's own Son. "The only one that can give us life," He shed His blood to make my sins white as snow.

A jolt like electricity buckled my knees and I toppled from the stool. The words of the song paralleled what I had seen, and the reality of it hit me with the force of a tsunami—*God is real. Jesus is real. He is fearsomely and wonderfully real, and I saw Him face-to-face.*

I had been allowed to witness Him in the throes of the greatest act of love ever performed in the history of the cosmos, the act that defies nature, confounds reason—the cross.

But what did this mean? What was I to do with it?

A compulsion enveloped me, gentle but at the same time strong and majestic. The faint voice that had called to me through the whip-poor-will nine years earlier wooed me once more. The summons that had beckoned from the depths of the agate. It drew me with a gentle whisper robust and noble, igniting my soul.

"Come to the wilderness!"

The mystery over the treetops would at last be revealed. The treasure! The source of the ecstasy! The secret would now burst forth!

Inebriated by the voice, my consciousness went into suspension. Barely aware of myself, my legs propelled me down the stairs and out the door. I ran. Over the hill behind the airstrip and into the forest my feet carried me. Neither direction nor destiny were of concern. The voice drew me, a magnet, an unseen hand leading me to the secret place where Mystery's light at last would expose the long-sequestered rune.

My feet reached a grassy clearing deep among the trees, secluded from human eyes. The pull of the magnet dwindled. Peace enveloped me. My sneakers padded to a halt.

What would happen now?

A mossy log invited me to sit. There in the stillness of nature I closed my eyes. My breathing slowed. From deep within I listened again for that sweet but mighty voice.

For a long moment my ears carried to my brain the proximity of chirping birds and scampering of an occasional squirrel or breath of wind rustling the tree branches.

Then I sensed a presence. Mystery had drawn near. Mystery would now speak.

An ancient door swung open to a long-sealed cavern, and a beam of light fell on unspeakable riches.

The experience in all its holy passion and inebriating wonder flooded back.

The memory of The Dream returned.

But it no longer stood alone. Now it exceeded the definition of a memory or even of an experience. Now it made sense. I saw the connection.

In the awe and shock of the revelation, my body emitted an involuntary gasp and I found myself reeling, slipping from the log into the grassy leaves below.

The man lives! The lovely man exists!

Last night He had visited me. Not in a subliminal out-of-body vision, but for real. He had touched me. I had touched Him. He had spoken with me.

Now at last I knew His name.

The man's name was Jesus.

The Dream had been no fantasy, but a prophetic revelation of Divine Love. To free the captives He had yielded Himself to torture and death—made ragged so others might be redeemed. This holy love, this selfless beauty, was the priceless treasure beyond the treetops, that for which my soul had yearned even from early childhood, dreadful yet lovely.

The veil was also lifted from Mystery. The voice that had entreated me from the whip-poor-will and the agate. Mystery was His Spirit, by whom the man would interact with His bride. In the form of that Spirit, He was there beside me, sitting on the log with His arm around my shoulders.

What I had experienced last night had consummated our union. He had chosen me . . . and not only me, but anyone who hears the call of the whip-poor-will, the call to embrace the treasure of His love. For the rest of eternity my Beloved and I would rollick together in blessed and holy romance.

From that point I embarked on life in a different realm. Now each day offered new discoveries and challenges in union with Him. My Beloved embodied the pinnacle of gentleness, kindness, selflessness, purity—holiness. To bring Him joy by emulating Him and reflecting as a miniature light His radiant characteristics eclipsed all other goals and comprised my sole pursuit.

But such lofty chastity was as foreign to me as Mars. Having barged through life as a feral jungle rat for fifteen years, I now found myself in the courts of the King. Bull in a china shop, so to speak. Learning curve ahead!

Kingdom Citizenship 101 involved vanquishing my potty mouth and sewer brain through which flowed profanity, rebellion against my parents, vengeful thoughts against kids I didn't like in school and a continuous stream of selfishness. The passion for my Beloved, now a roaring blowtorch in my soul, declared war on all that was not aligned with Him. Day by day a new me grew inside my will and thoughts. It did ferocious combat with the old carnal me, which fought back with the fury of a cornered jackal. But readily a prayer away, my Beloved stood by, encouraging me, guiding me, His very presence turning it all into a joyous adventure. Slowly, through relentless onslaught the old me with its dirty thoughts and selfish acts reluctantly withered away, and I became a new creation, a queen walking in victory with my King.

Mom experienced a vision of Christ soon after I did, on Easter Sunday morning. Now she, too, burned with zeal for God. Poor Dad, ever and faithfully protective of "his girls," couldn't understand what had happened to us. Why did his wife and daughter now hanker to attend church whenever the doors were open? Why had the Bible permanently left its safe, dusty spot on the bottommost bookshelf and, displacing my horse books and Mom's gardening magazines, usurped prime territory front and center of every desk and table?

"That church brainwashed my family! It made them into religious nuts!" was the conclusion he drew. So Dad forbade me to read the Bible or go to church except on Sundays. To be caught reading the Bible when Dad entered the house from the shop was sure to result in a shouting tirade generously decorated with four-letter words.

Church I could do without, but not the Bible. The new baby me possessed an insatiable appetite for God's Word, and would not be deterred from ingesting it.

Opposition can have two effects on a vision. If the fire of vision and passion is weak, it can have the effect of water poured on a smoldering pile of garbage. With a hiss and a sizzle and a wisp of smoke, the fire is gone, not to be relit except with much effort.

But if the fire has come up from a burning oil well deep within, even a mile-deep ocean pressing down from above has no effect. A fire hose turned on a volcano is likely to produce fossilized firefighters. The fire licks up the water and grows stronger. The wind of opposition fans it to greater heights until it consumes whatever bars its path.

The treasure was no longer a mystery, but a living, pulsing, glorious adventure. The romance had become real. Neither harsh words nor violent threats could contain this raging inferno blasting up from deep within my soul. But there was no reasoning with Dad, so I found another way.

Procuring tracing paper and a fine nib pen, I smuggled a Bible outside and hid it in the weeds half-underneath the edge of a massive boulder between the house and the horse barn. There at varying intervals and at times least suspected by Dad, I stole to copy, in microscopic handwriting, those select verses that I felt were key to understanding, knowing and following my Beloved.

Once complete, I could easily hide my tiny stripped-down Bible between the pages of a schoolbook or a horse magazine. According to tradition, evenings were family time. Mom sat in the rocking chair and Dad sat on one end of the couch watching TV and I sat on the other end of the couch doing homework or studying horse books. To remove myself from my spot for more than a few minutes would have evoked inquiry, because this was how the Cinquanta family had spent our evenings since forever.

To open a Bible in this environment was unthinkable, because the entire evening would be made miserable with a ranting, raving Dad decrying the assumed evils of churches, pastors and others whom he deemed to be hypocrites. But now, right there under Dad's nose, I could freely study the Bible. If he glanced my way or moved too close I nonchalantly flipped a page of the horse magazine or schoolbook, completely concealing the handmade Bible.

This mild persecution provoked me to best it by leveraging greater resourcefulness than just copying verses into a semi-invisible manuscript. I created a tiny cheat sheet with one- or two-word clues based on which I began to memorize the verses I had copied. Within a year I had internalized copious blocks of Scripture. This proved an invaluable tool later on.

Though I was oblivious to its workings, Mystery's agenda for me included more shocking collisions, and for these I was being prepared. The Encounter had launched my transformation and set sail to this adventure with my Beloved. With that I assumed the full trove of treasure had been found. This relationship we now enjoyed surely embodied the summation of the Mystery, the consummation of resplendent wonder and divine beauty. I supposed the seas ahead to be glassy and golden, my life an endless ballet of tranquility and bliss with my Beloved Lord.

But I was mistaken. The path toward my destiny had only commenced. The treasure's complete manifestation had not yet been revealed. Mystery's wisdom concealed from me certain dangerous knowledge—for the unearthing of that deep buried treasure would cost me everything.

3

Into Darkness

Treasure does not drop from the sky
Nor is it found on a leisurely stroll.
Treasure lies hidden in darkness
Concealed beneath oceans or imprisoned
   within rock.
That soul only shall bring it forth
Who values it more than life
And who dares risk all to find it.

Dread Commission

Throughout my college years, Dad and Mom tirelessly labored to set their daughter up for a bright future. Having purchased twenty acres of land north of Minneapolis, they set out to build for me an equestrian's dream facility—a free-span steel riding arena measuring two hundred feet long and seventy feet wide with attached house and stable, and an outdoor arena and pastures, all debt-free. To earn the money for the project Dad repaired or modified airplanes for customers, and with each paycheck bought great quantities of steel for the roof and massive wooden beams for the upright posts and angle iron for the trusses. Then he welded and dug and pounded, all with his own hands, while Mom kept food on the table by waitressing.

Meanwhile Dad's own dream—his ornithopter—rusted away in a swamp. Health failing, he had resigned himself to the conviction that if not he then no one would gain access to his ingenious hydraulic joint and crack the mystery of how to build a real man-powered flapping-wing aircraft. Rather than risk it being pirated and patented by others, he chose to let it go to ruin.

Now the arena, the greatest architectural undertaking of my parents' tireless conquest of the impossible, had consumed five of his elder years . . . and at long last it was complete, perfectly timed to serve as my college graduation gift. Equipped with a debt-free facility ready to be used, his daughter could now rise to equestrian greatness.

My future was secure.

But as I laid my gown in a drawer and watched Mom proudly hang my honor stole and tassel on the wall with my freshly framed graduation photo, I knew I could not yet plunge headlong into my horse career.

The voice of my Beloved called to me.

Seven years had passed since the treasure of the lovely man had been revealed, and I embarked on an adventure in holy romance with the One who had broken the power of

106

darkness. Throughout this time He had nurtured me and we had romped together, laughed together and cried together, and I had discovered deeper depths of His beauty.

Yet I knew our relationship was not an end in itself, but preparation for an unknown quest. I thought, with full confidence, that I knew what that "quest" entailed; along with continuing the pursuit of my equestrian career, I would minister to college students.

During my first year in college the church elders had noted my flaming passion for God and selected me to serve as one of two student leaders of the church's campus ministry. Thus I had been graced with the thrill of leading other students to receive Jesus' love and new life. I had helped new believers discover their spiritual gifts, written and then taught dramas and plays and choreographed dances and ignited robust debates by opposing the college newspaper's atheistic columnist with articles in defense of the Bible. While others partied on Friday nights, a radical remnant of us hit the streets looking for opportunities to pray with people. During one of these outings I had received a prophetic revelation that resulted in saving a girl who was on her way to commit suicide by throwing herself from a nearby bridge.

These being a scant few of the adventures enlivening my college years, I felt certain my future held continuing activities on college campuses, bringing Jesus' love to searching students though I had acquired my tassel and sash.

But I had undergone no Bible training. My instruction in the things of the Spirit included sermons heard in church and the rich training my Beloved Himself had provided through the Bible and His voice quietly, gently guiding and teaching me day by day. But now His voice said, "You must receive Bible training."

So I informed my parents of my wish to enroll in a Bible course, assuring them, "When the six-month course is over, I'll come back home and start using the facility to train horses."

Research and circumstances narrowed the options to two Bible schools and then one: Youth With A Mission in Denver, Colorado.

Youth With A Mission epitomized a little piece of heaven on earth. Surrounded by others my age who craved to rescue a hurting world, I imbibed Spirit-empowered worship and intriguing teachings from the Bible. Our training included carrying a cross down the street in the city's red-light district and getting mocked and spat on, performing dramas on street corners and learning to hear the Lord's voice for prophetic insights.

But Mystery would break in on me once more. What I had received so far had laid the groundwork. The purpose for which I had been born, in all its wonder and terror, had now come ripe to be revealed. The second part of the treasure swathed in darkness would now manifest.

Friday was movie night. My peers and I grabbed our junk food and hunkered down in the sofa or on pillows, and the show commenced.

Not five minutes passed before an aura completely unrelated and external to the environment of the room rushed over me. The world began to spin. An overwhelming, all-eclipsing voice pounded through my soul, a massive drum in the middle of my body. It boomed, *"God wants to say something to you"*—a summons from my Beloved.

So strong hammered the drum I feared my chest would explode. My Beloved had never spoken to me this way. He must have an extremely urgent message. Desperate to find a quiet location and learn what manner of edict this might be, I fled the room. My sudden exit alarmed my comrades, who must have assumed me to be suffering a case of diarrhea.

Grabbing my Bible I planted myself in a chair in the corner of a deserted hallway. Breathless, I asked, "What do You want to tell me?"

His voice rolled into my spirit as clear as if a person were standing there speaking. *"I'm sending you to the unreached nations."*

In our classes the instructors had taught on the topic "Unreached Nations"—places in the world where people still had no access to the knowledge of Jesus. They lived out their whole lives, generation after generation, with no Dave or Phil to demonstrate Christ to them, no one to share the liberating message of forgiveness and new life. These same nations and peoples were steeped in poverty, plagued by war, oppressed by ungodly governments and denied the education and justice that could bring them a hope and a future.

Twice had I ventured beyond the fifty states: In Mexico at age seven I devoured the most yummy tamale on earth while a sombrero bigger than my body kept falling over my eyes to the delight of my adoring parents.

Then, on an outing to London with my teetotaling college ministry group, I learned that "root beer" to a British waiter translates into a frothing mug of Carlsberg.

Though grand adventures, I returned from these outings with two firm conclusions: The good ol' U.S. of A. is the best place on Planet Earth, and for the duration of my sojourn on said Planet Earth, I would be most content to remain beneath her spacious skies. One lone exception to this resolution had fluttered across my gray matter. Magazines picturing breathtaking European horses dancing across dressage arenas ignited a desire to someday take a jaunt to Germany, source of the most splendid equines in the world.

But . . . the unreached nations? One of those desolate, godforsaken, barbaric jungles on the back side of the planet? I was supposed to go there? Unfathomable!

I had come to know the voice of my Beloved Lord. Through all our talks in the wilderness His voice had not once come to me with such absolute certitude. Nevertheless, something must surely be wrong! *I must be mistaken. I cannot be hearing correctly. This must be a mistake.*

"Lord, uh . . . this has to be a joke. Tell me this is a joke," I argued. "If this is You talking to me, then give me confirmation."

That will be the end of it, I thought. *Nothing will happen.* Wrong.

Instantly the same voice resounded, *Turn to Ezekiel chapter thirty-six, start at verse twenty-four.*

Ezekiel!? Ezekiel was a book in the Bible, buried someplace in the Old Testament, but I had certainly not read it. Flipping through the pages, I found Ezekiel. Chapter 36? *There's probably not even that many chapters*, I thought. But there were. With a mixture of angst and awe, I read from verse 24.

"I will take you out of the nations; I will gather you from all the countries and bring you back into your own land. . . ."

In the ancient times when that was written, the people had been conquered by a powerful kingdom. They were now captives in a faraway land. Their subjugators followed dark practices and didn't adhere to the morals or ways of God. The people longed to return to their own land. They longed for freedom, and God promised to rescue them.

The passage continued, "*I will sprinkle clean water on you, and you will be clean; I will cleanse you from all your impurities and from all your idols. . . .*"

When I read the word *idols*, the Lord spoke again: *I'm sending you to a land of idolatry to bring My people out.*

My brain froze. *What?* Not only a faraway, unreached nation, but also an idolatrous nation? He was definitely not referring to Germany, and I could be certain that "bring My people out" had nothing to do with exporting fine horses! I knew what missionaries were, but that work wasn't for me. I would finish this Bible school and return home to the beautiful facility Dad had built for me. I would train horses, and on the side I would minister to college students as I had for the past four years. So I already knew the manner of my service for God . . . or did I?

I could not deny that my Beloved was talking to me— loud and clear! The unreached nations of which our instructor had taught us paraded through my mind, each replacing a horse on a great cosmic merry-go-round. "*Idolatrous nation . . .*" To which idolatrous nation did God want me to go?

Africa rose up before me, surging upward high into the sky. Was I to go to Africa? Out of the continent burst black-skinned, minimally clothed tribals with dreadful piercings and scarification, performing a wild dance to deafening drumbeats. Then Africa split into its nations. Each on a pole. Up-down, 'round and 'round spun the merry-go-round. Dizzying. Was I supposed to go to a nation in Africa?

Indonesia jumped onto the merry-go-round, followed by New Guinea and Sri Lanka and Fiji and Haiti. Jungle animals screeched and hooted and howled while brown-legged savages dashed about brandishing primitive wooden spears with which they gored wild boars and each other. Was I to go to an island out in the middle of the ocean?

Tibet and Mongolia joined the melee, with yaks and snow and barren tundra moonscapes and Buddhist flags and temples. Was it someplace up north?

Then came India. It took its place on the merry-go-round, one gigantic nation towering above the rest, painted orange and green and white.

Our instructor's words rang in my ears. "India," he had said, "is one of the greatest unreached mission frontiers. Its population is over a billion. That means one out of five people in the world lives in India."

India began to crawl. Its surface churned. Not like a wave, but like millions of tiny individual bodies dashing in different directions. A seething, ghastly anthill.

My fondness for a multiplicity of critters did not extend to ants. Ever since they had crawled up my pants when I was a little girl in Washington, ants gave me the heebie-jeebies. Later in Arizona, I remembered great barren circles, perfectly round, in which not a single blade of grass or shrub dared to grow. In the middle of the circle lived a colony of vicious red ants. The ants were my enemies. I tiptoed close enough to poke a stick down there, and out of the hole poured thousands of furious six-legged warriors. Jaws gaping, they swarmed out ready to elicit excruciating pain on whatever had dared invade their territory. Within seconds the terrain around their hole vanished beneath a living, expanding black-red swarm. Trotting backward, I maintained a few inches' gap between my toes and the advancing horde and taunted, "Come on, try to bite me!" Once one did. The unforgettable searing pain of a split-second flesh-in-jaws relationship with a fire ant would forever clinch my lifelong aversion to the little beasties.

112

At that moment, they constituted the closest dynamic equivalent to the millions of people seething across India.

"Around seventy-four percent follow Hinduism and twenty percent Islam," the instructor had continued. "In each state they speak a different language. But that's not all. They have different dialects. Upon crossing into a different county, the dialect changes. So the language barrier is formidable."

Now the seething human blanket running helter-skelter across India began to speak. Each sector emitted a different stream of unintelligible gibberish. The cacophony rose as a rustling upsurged to a roar and then crescended to a din of total confusion.

"Then," the instructor had continued, "there's idol worship. Since ancient times the people have held superstitions and alleviated their fear of the unknown by invoking innumerable gods and goddesses. The official count is 330 million distinct deities that are revered, feared and appeased."

Images peppered the moving blanket across India, some grotesque, some comical, others dreadful demons. Man-made fetishes decked with gold and rubies but lifeless, powerless. The roaring, cacophonic voices methodized into ritual chanting and cries for deliverance and prayers for help and healing and peace, millions of brown faces prostrate before gods fashioned by their own hands. The prayers fell unheard. They dropped into the emptiness of space, wasted. The idols remained unmoved, cold sentinels over a nation in slavery. The blanket of moving, seething humanity morphed into a midnight-deep, empty dark void, the soul-state of millions searching in the wrong places for their Creator.

"Some of the worst poverty imaginable plagues this nation," the instructor had continued. "Of around seventy-five million children, many are orphaned or malnourished.

Thousands are trafficked into the sex trade. Over fifty percent have little access to education. In the unreached north alone, thirty-five million children face a dismal future of recycling the misery of their parents."

A tar-like blackness now blotted out the green and orange and white colors of India, seeping, creeping, obliterating everything in its path. The dreadful tar terminated the movement of the wailing humanity until the whole nation was encased, frozen in a cocoon of death.

"So," concluded the instructor, "India is one of the most difficult mission fields in the world."

No duh. That settled it. One decision I would not have to make. Of all the nations of the world, I was NOT going to India!

Other nations qualifying as "idolatrous" and "unreached" presented themselves, but I hardly noticed them. Their visage was eclipsed by the afterimage of India—seething masses, empty cries and hopeless eyes and the blackness, reaching out to drag the people into destruction.

No way. Not going to India! Plenty of other places to go. But what about my horse career? What about campus ministry? What about Dad, who had just completed the splendid facility for me, for my future? What nonsense was this anyway?

My Beloved desired that I help rescue people in an unreached, idolatrous place. But where? The merry-go-round of nations trampled me, drug me. Maps and cities and people's faces, black and yellow and red, swirled above, below, around.

For one weird, confusing moment I was caught in an ambiguous whirlwind. This whole idea of leaving America was so outrageous, so foreign. Everything I had planned for my life, everything I had thought I was going to do, everything

I had prepared for, was now being threatened, torn up by the roots.

One certainty I would cling to. One place I could not live, one act I would not do for God. Of all those crazy places that had passed before my eyes . . . fine, okay, I would go. I would do that for God. But one place I would not go.

From the midst of the whirlwind I soundlessly screamed my resolution.

I'll go anyplace but India!

Then, bursting through the confusion, came His voice, calm, firm, matter-of-fact.

"Start in India."

BAM!

The merry-go-round ended. The room stopped swirling. The nations and maps and tribals and spears and drums fizzled into oblivion. For one moment I reeled like a dizzy kid who fell off the merry-go-round horse and tried to see where Mommy was in the crowd.

Then I realized . . . something had changed.

When I looked out at the horizon of my life ahead, I no longer saw magnificent horses dancing across manicured arenas. All ambition to make a career of horse training that had filled my world mere moments ago, was gone. With it my zeal for campus ministry had also vanished.

From that moment, a profoundly different future rose on the horizon of my life. It filled my vision, all-encompassing, obliterating every other thought, care or aspiration. A searing passion, an excitement weighed with sobriety, a joy tempered with trepidation, surged through my every cell and sinew.

INDIA! I must liberate the captives in India! My Beloved died and rose again for their freedom. He has prepared me for this destiny. I must bring His people out of bondage!

That night I lay on my bed in a daze. The following morning at breakfast I was stunned to discover that our guest speaker for the entire upcoming week was the director of outreaches to India. Then out of the 150 or so students and staff whose names had gone into a hat to see who would be granted the intense privilege of sitting at the head table with the guest speaker, mine had been drawn.

After two days I knew exactly what I must do. The act to be undertaken would be neither a pretty sight nor a happy occasion. It would be the most difficult act I'd ever carried out, akin to mercy-killing a beloved pet that had run out in the road and had half its body mangled by a car. There was no question and no other option. The knife must fall and it must fall swiftly.

I must tell Dad.

When you have to carry out a traumatic and painful act, moments last years. I remember each stair step as I descended the half-flight from the main level of the building. There, occupying a subterranean cubbyhole in the hallway, was the pay phone. When I picked up the receiver, I knew this was the irreversible first step toward the unknown darkness into which the voice of my Beloved called me. The words I must deliver into that receiver would seal the direction of the rest of my life.

Each coin dropping into the slot was a piece of my former life being cast down, a sacrifice laid before God, irretrievably and irrevocably abandoned. All that was familiar, comfortable and safe now vanished into the pay phone slot.

The gentle blowing of air against my cheek from the nostrils of a horse giving a kiss in the only way it can. The vibrant power of its muscles rippling beneath my seat and legs, its mouth pulsing in my fingertips as we danced across a dressage arena.

Clink.

Gone. Cast away. Sacrificed.

The suicidal college student whose distress turned to joy when I testified of Jesus' love, how He was longing to give her hope and a future. Would I ever minister to another young person in that way?

Clink.

Maybe. Maybe not. That was now up to God. He was calling me in a different direction.

America, with its blessings and efficiency and beauty. My voyages to other lands, even "nice" places in the world, had confirmed my pleasure to forever remain betwixt her resplendent shores.

Clink.

Gone. Relinquished. Now I was headed for the wilds of an undeveloped nation racked with poverty and disease and superstition . . . and seething with ant-like hordes of humanity. Life from now on would not include much comfort and might be downright terrifying.

Then the phone was ringing in my parents' house. Who would pick up, Mom? Or Dad? I hoped Dad, for then I could get this over with quickly.

"Hello?"

Shucks. "Hi, Mom."

"Oh, hi, honey! How's it going?"

I was shaking. Would my anxiety also come through in my voice? I must make this brief. "Everything's fine. Can I talk to Dad?"

"Sure, he's outside. Let me call him."

Mom set the phone down and I could hear her going out. I took a deep breath and rehearsed for the umpteenth time the words I intended to speak, but each time they came through differently.

"He'll be right in."

Mom again. Bummer. I'd have to talk to her.

"So what 'cha been learning?"

"Uh . . . nothing much." I had to make conversation. What could I talk about to kill time? "Last weekend we found this great hill to go sledding on. We were having a blast and then guess what? The cops arrived!"

"Oh gosh, why?" queried Mom.

"Well, it was posted 'No Trespassing,' but we hadn't seen the sign because it was way high up on a telephone pole. So we snapped our photo in front of the squad car with the cop before leaving the premises."

"Okay, glad everything turned out okay. Here's Dad."

Fumble, fumble . . . the handset being transferred to Dad.

"Hi, sweetie, what's up?"

"Hi, Dad." My palms were dripping wet, and my heart pounded in my throat. For one split second I desired to run. To stop, to go the other way, to forget this had happened. The knife was poised at the throat of my terminally wounded pet, ready to carry out the dreaded execution. . . .

"Uh, Dad, there's something I have to tell you."

"Sure. Is everything okay?"

"Yeah, of course. But, um . . . well, I . . ." It was now or never. Then I blurted it out. *"I'm going to India. I'm not coming back to train horses. Sell the horse facility."*

The dagger had fallen. The excruciating act had been carried out.

On the other end of the phone . . . silence.

I waited.

Dad could be vociferous when displeased, so certainly the eye of the hurricane was upon me. Any second the lull would be shattered by a tirade.

Instead, the unexpected and unbelievable happened.
Click.
Dad had hung up the phone.

I stood there staring aghast at the dead handset. Not once in my life had my parents hung up the phone on me or refused to speak to me. But it was also entirely justified. I had killed Dad's dream.

To fund and facilitate my equestrian future, Dad had sacrificed his own dream of being the first to build a functional ornithopter. Now his sacrifice was rendered pointless, a waste. Moreover, five years of hard labor building the arena had ruined what had remained of his failing health.

He had poured his whole life into setting me up for a great future pursuing what had been my dream. In his youth he had to struggle, with no one to encourage or help him. Possessing no money for a ticket, he had come nigh to suffocation while hoboing on top of the old coal trains. Upon arriving at his destination, he had had to start from zero, working and earning a living though only fifteen years old. Wicked men had tried to misuse him. Others had taken advantage of him in an era when the offspring of Italian immigrants faced racial discrimination.

Dad envisioned a more serene and prosperous life for his daughter. He had invested the last ounce of his strength and wealth to set me up so I wouldn't have to struggle. He had given up his own dream to make mine a reality.

And now, I had abandoned it. Having at last completed his work, looking forward to sitting back and watching his daughter run on the platform he'd created, I was forsaking it and heading off in a different direction.

In Dad's eyes, going to India meant becoming a missionary. He understood missionaries to be poor wretches who were so hopelessly brainwashed as to squander their lives trying to help people who didn't deserve help, people who refused to help themselves. In his perception, I had doomed myself to a life of dishonor and deprivation. In his eyes I'd once been a respectable young professional heading for an illustrious career, but now he perceived my decision on par with throwing it all away for the undignified path of a beggar living on handouts. To a loving father, it was a devastating blow.

Thus the tears I fought back as I hung up the receiver weren't from self-pity or a sense of rejection or abandonment or anything having to do with myself. I grieved for my dad's broken heart.

Little did I know that the decision I made that day—to abandon all and follow Mystery's call into the dark unknown of India—constituted a declaration of war. Had I rejected the call and continued the pursuit of my happy little life in my own way and my own direction, the governors of Sheol would not have cast me another glance. I would not have posed a threat. But the call had overcome me, and I had cast myself headlong into it. Now Mystery would show me a graphic glimpse of the goings-on in the epicenter of spiritual darkness, India's Mordor.

Shadow of the Fortress

Soaring high above the earth as if in a spaceship, I looked down on the blue-white swirls of cloud and sea, and beyond at the blackness of outer space speckled with stars. But no man-made craft enclosed me, and there was no visible means of conveyance.

The arc of my travel curved downward. I was drawn closer and closer to the earth. Continents and oceans materialized. The Americas passed below, and then Europe and the Middle East. My direction turned northward and I passed over the massive expanses of China and Russia.

From there I was carried southward. Ahead I could see the mighty Himalayas, their white peaks a great barrier between north and south. Below stretched the green-brown lands of India, Bangladesh, Pakistan. The Ganges River coursed its way past Delhi, across the whole northern part of India to Calcutta, a blue-green serpent slithering across the land.

Then I noticed something abnormal. Though the sun was high, a dark shadow stretched across the whole land of India, Pakistan and Bangladesh. The shadow was cast from the region of the mountains and the Ganges River, but it wasn't a physical shadow. The shadow was alive. Like a wind carrying in its wake the spores of a deadly disease, the shadow bore an ominous sense of darkness and sorrow.

Then the mountains began to move! Mighty rocks shifted and changed shape. Cliffs cracked and stretched, creating sheer drops thousands of feet high. The white peaks rose higher and higher into a sky boiling with angry vapors shot through with bolts of lightning. The peaks themselves morphed and sharpened, thrusting high and higher into the heavens, spears raised for war.

In an instant the transformation was complete. What now stood before my wondering eyes were not mountains but a vast kingdom. The Himalayas had become castles, a mighty army of turrets and bulwarks composing one colossal fortress stretching from above Pakistan eastward to the middle of China.

The castles weren't built of hewn stone with walls and moats and battlements and chivalrous knights in shining armor. Molded of solid metamorphic rock, without a seam or joint, a colossal sculpture fashioned from molten lava, they pulsed forth waves of darkness. Rather than a place to house and protect royalty, these castles conveyed an aura of dread, as if formed by unearthly powers and charmed with an evil omen. What once were snow-covered peaks had become white flags flying from the pinnacles of dagger-point spires.

Hewn into the sheer stone surface of the spires, half-concealed by the suffocating darkness and whirling vapors, sullen empty windows gaped black and foreboding. Intertwined in mutual conspiracy, the fortress and the raging storm above discharged an icy wind out across the defenseless lands lying to the south—namely, India.

Carried along by an invisible, unfelt, unseen force, I was taken to the base of one of the great spires. Then, with one blast of thrust as if poised on the tip of a rocket, I was propelled upward, up and up along the vertical surface, molded stone and hollow windows whizzing past inches from my body. Up, up, into dense and violent weather.

Then my transport stopped.

I was looking into one of those gaping openings in the spire, a cavern into a void, a porthole into the heart of the mountain. I hung in midair, staring transfixed. If the halt had exceeded a split second, I would have screamed, "No way, I'm not going in there!"

Then I was inside. Before me stood a creature that rendered Godzilla a featherweight. Its massive, iron-armored shoulders loomed high into the cavernous interior of the spire. It had a man-like face but by no means was it human. It had no neck, its head rising directly out of its shoulders. Deep lines crevassed its leathered face, and dead skin, flaking and cracking, hung from the sides of its nose and the corners of its eyes and from the folds where its chin joined its chest. Wiry hair protruded in odd places, scraggly, some black, some gray. The creature conveyed the image of primeval archaism, having stood rooted for millennia, right here in this same spot, since the beginning of time.

Planted firmly on the creature's head rode a golden crown studded with colored stones. Behind it stood a golden throne adorned with intricate sculpting and inlaid gems. But the throne was at the same time a chariot. Golden wheels studded with rubies bounded either side. I puzzled over why a throne would also be a chariot.

The creature stood in a crouched position, feet planted for combat. It was intent on a task, and its expression bespoke a mix of engrossment and pride. Facing one of the great voids in the citadel wall that afforded a clear overlook to the plains below, the creature's yellow cougar's teeth clenched in combined effort and elation.

Its gnarled fists gripped massive iron chains, rough and rusty black. One link alone spanned the breadth of a man's hand. My attention was drawn to the manner in which the creature gripped the chains. Coiled in a great mound on the floor of the cavern, the chains swooped up and up, spanning the full height of the creature's massive frame. They passed from the bottom of its fists and out between its thumbs and forefingers, as a coachman would grip reins when driving a horse-drawn cart. But reins of chain? Reins consist of leather, not chain. So, what could this mean?

If the creature represented a king or ruler, one might expect to see a scepter in its hand. Indeed, at that moment I saw that the creature held a tool in its fist. It wasn't a scepter, but a bullwhip. Crouching with bent knees as if perched upon a speeding chariot, the king-cum-charioteer bellowed a roar of pleasure and yanked the chains and snapped the whip, and the storm raging above echoed with a crack of lightning and an extra-strong gust of wind.

A compelling question pounded in my mind: *What is at the end of the reins? Is the creature driving horses? Or something else?*

With that I was propelled back out through the opening, southward, again facing north and viewing the spires of the fortress that had been the Himalayas. Now I saw that the creature I had visited was not riding solitaire. A similar warlord manned each spire. Crowned with power, brandishing whips for scepters, they gripped iron reins as if driving chariots. Together they formed a mighty army. When one roared the whole land trembled and the black clouds boiled and a fresh gust of icy wind tore out past the spires and swept across the land.

What is at the end of the chains? The dread question banged in my brain like cymbals.

From the pinnacle of the spires, from the black void that marked the place where the creatures stood and overlooked the land below, the great chains descended and fanned out. I was carried along them, plunging down and down toward the plains below the mountains.

Then I saw the river. Tar-black, it wound across the land, a great slough from which arose a black mist and the stench of death. But in the occasional shaft of light penetrating the swirling storm, its blackness gave way to an eerie but beautiful silver-green. The reflection of the light upon the river carried with it a tremor of hope, the faint cry, a victim calling for help.

But no sooner did the light touch upon the river and the pulse of hope go forth, than the dark clouds closed over it, a criminal violently gagging his victim. The river was again swathed in blackness.

Stationed in the wide floodplain along the bank of the river towered more of the same fearsome creatures. The chains they held joined the others from the spires above, doubling their strength, extending their reach.

Then faintly at first but growing in volume I heard voices. Wails and cries of misery, sadness and suffering. Sounds of fear and anguish and longing and oppression. The wails amplified, sending chills down my spine. I was seized by an overwhelming impulse to escape, to rewind, to flee from the whole experience. But there was no escape. I was carried on, down and down the length of the chain, closer and closer to the earth, nearer to the voices and the river.

At last I reached the end of the chain.

There, sitting in her own urine, a naked baby girl reached out a besoiled hand. Flies congregated on her tear-encrusted eyes and parched lips. No one was there to brush them away; no one was there to care. Weakened by malnutrition, her sobs came in choking gasps. The iron chain wound around her, a spiritual python. It represented neglect, deprivation and starvation. Slowly, painfully, it was strangling her. The chain began to pull her into the greasy green-gray waters of the Ganges. Then she looked at me. Her dull, matted eyes grew wide and for one moment shone with hope. Her tiny hand reached toward me. Reached into my heart and took hold of it.

Broken with compassion, I reached out to take her in my arms, comfort her, wipe away the tears and the flies, feed, clothe, nurture her. . . .

But instantly I was transported and found myself at the end of another chain. A thin man toiled alone in a field, hacking at parched ground with a primitive shovel. Ragged trousers, threadbare shirt and sandal soles worn paper-thin attested to his hand-to-mouth subsistence. His eyes were empty and hopeless, his future doomed to inescapable misery. The chain formed shackles on his wrists and ankles encumbering and limiting his mobility. The chain represented crushing poverty, oppressive creditors and a cruel system of culturally approved slavery.

Far across the plain one of the warlords roared in glee. He jerked the chain and cracked a whip and the shackles tightened around the man's limbs. Blood oozed out where they cut into his flesh, and with each move the torture increased. Still, driven by the hungry eyes of his children in the hut nearby, he labored on.

Rage seized me. I could not let this continue. *I must stop this man's suffering. I must liberate him from this slavery.* Oblivious to reason I lunged forward to grab hold of the chain.

At that moment I was again transported. A brightly clad woman tenderly held in her palm a bowl made of dried leaves. She appeared middle-class—robust of body, adorned with gold and bracelets and a modern purse on her shoulder. Fishing in another bag she had set on the ground, she struck a match and from within the bowl a candle flamed.

Before her stood the image of an elephant. It was humanoid, obese, with blank eyes staring emptily into space, and seated on a throne, bedecked with jewels. In one hand it held a scepter. The woman laid the offerings before the plastic and clay image, and prayed for protection and salvation and peace for her family. But there was no peace in her face, only fear. There was no joy, only pain. The chain that bound her passed not only around its victim but inside, penetrating her body. It bound her to the idol, and then it reversed and entered her again, multiplying her fear, increasing her pain, inspiring more longing for freedom, peace, joy and salvation.

I was then whisked up again to a height as if flying a small plane. From there I could see that the whole land was shackled in these chains, millions of people bound and enslaved by the creatures who stood as minions in the castles and the plains. A great moaning ascended from them, a longing for freedom, for hope, for a future. High in the castles and along the river, the creatures leered and gloated, knowing their vassals could never be free, unable to escape the power of their chains.

The dream ended.

The following night, I saw the exact same dream.

The third night, the same dream occurred again.

Then I knew. It was not to the lush jungles of southern India that I must go. It was not to the plateau-lands of the central regions where tribals roamed. It was not to the great city of Bombay, nor to the coastal areas of Orissa or Goa.

My assignment targeted the root of the people's pain. I must go to the source of the problem and liberate those under the immediate shadow of oppression.

Doubt and questions were annihilated. I had glimpsed the spiritual government that bound one-fifth of the world in slavery to poverty, disease and fear. I had glimpsed what the Bible means by principalities, powers and rulers of darkness in high places described in Ephesians 6:12. These bogus kings, whose interest is to kill, steal and destroy, were trespassers. The true King—the One who created all matter, who loved us so intensely as to give His life for us, my Beloved—longed to set free His creation, which groaned under their rule. But whom would He send?

Now I knew. He was sending me. He was showing me that the northern area, the region of the Himalayas and the Ganges River, was the key to the nation. His strategy was to attack the stronghold and set the prisoners free. But to take back this segment of the planet and reestablish His reign of justice and freedom, He would not act independently. He had chosen to use the weakness of humanity to show His strength.

He was appointing me to join His mission.

From then on a singular passion consumed me. *I must prepare myself for the battle ahead.* Day after day, as an athlete training for the match, I could be found in the library devouring every scrap of intelligence available regarding the land beneath the mighty Himalayas.

Research confirmed that northern India was one of the most needy and oppressed places in the world, with hundreds of millions surviving on less than one dollar a day. Witch doctors performed incantations and prescribed potions that left their patients sicker than before. Loan sharks held the landless in slavery to debt. The bogus kings and their chains and whips represented poverty and disease, and the spiritual government that gave it rise.

The people were steeped in centuries and generations of idol worship. Tradition and social pressure combined with no alternative revelation, leaving them desperately crying out to gods of stone and plastic and wood. A scant 0.1 percent of the population were followers of Jesus. In keeping with dictatorships, the spiritual government ruling from the North had hoodwinked them into the persuasion that their oppressors were benevolent gods to be worshiped.

I learned that in this northern region alone, 35 million orphan and destitute children faced a life of misery. Annually over 25 thousand girls succumbed to a hellish end as victims of sex trafficking, never again to see their families much less the light of freedom and dignity. The spiritual fortress along the mountains and bulwarked in the plains oversaw and fueled this business of soul mutilation.

I knew I must go to northern India and do battle against the warlords holding the people in bondage. They wielded chains and whips of poverty, oppression and disease. I wielded the name and authority of the rightful King who had "broken the power of darkness," the One who loved those people whom the warlords held in bondage, the One who had given His life for them and purchased their freedom with His own blood.

But that didn't mean victory would be easy or success ensured. Volumes have been written of those who forayed into formidable places on missions for the King and lost their lives. No books have been written about those who survived only to slink back to their homeland defeated and broken. Many of them endured unspeakable suffering and reaped scant reward. Would my mission end in the same defeat? What could one small woman do against the hordes of ancient evil enslaving hundreds of millions of people?

As my Beloved had given His life for me, now it was my turn to give mine for Him. This complete abandon to an impossible task could not have been originated by good intentions or by great vision. Love for Him was my sole motivator. And in that searing love, one conviction filled me with joy and anticipation and drove me onward toward the unknown. One all-consuming, inebriating and vivifying certitude:

I was not alone. He was with me . . . or rather, I was with Him. The heart of my Beloved broke for the desperate people in the shadow of the mountain. He was their rightful King, their Creator and Redeemer. But for millennia they had languished and cried, searching for hope with no one to guide them into His arms. The time had come. The King was now going forth to liberate His people, and I had been granted the privilege of joining His mission.

Mystery no longer wafted into my psyche as the faint call of a night bird. Mystery now pulsed within me, and I had yielded myself to serve as its vehicle executing its purpose in the world. Now I was teamed with Him, a dread and holy union of human and divine, breathing together, moving as one, my mind and body submitted in love-fired abandon to His Spirit and will.

Now the time had come to deploy and accomplish His purposes. Mystery now called me to go with Him into darkness, to liberate captives.

"Final call, Air India flight 635 to Delhi via Heathrow."

Mom released her long final embrace, and I leaned over to Dad, confined to a wheelchair by his advancing cancer. Tears welled up in his eyes. He reached out trembling arms with big hands still calloused from a lifetime of labor and enfolded me one last time. "Please . . . please take care of yourself, won't you?" He clung to me, caressing my shoulders, his lips quivering. "You're my little girl. You'll always be my little girl. Take care of yourself please!"

Though I had steeled myself for this moment, my throat burned with emotion. It was the first time in my life I'd seen Dad cry. I squeezed his hand and he clasped mine to his breast, desperate, unwilling to let go. "Sure, Dad, but get well, okay? When I come back I expect to see you stronger again and walking. I'll be fine, don't worry."

But I wasn't at all certain of what lay ahead for me and whether I would be fine or not. Reputed elders whose silver hairs attested wisdom far surpassing my 26 years had sternly warned, "You cannot go to north India alone. You must join a missionary organization and go with a group." They had recommended a plenteous spread of distinguished agencies that would welcome me and provide a base of support with fellow Americans to be my teammates. Others advised, "The people over there live differently than we do here in America. Their food will make you sick, and your body won't be able to withstand their unsanitary living conditions." One added, "What will happen to a petite young lady among those barbarians? You could disappear and nobody would be able to come to your rescue!"

Such words of negative encouragement had tested my resolve for weeks leading up to this day of embarkation. Was I this crazy? Didn't my Bible school certificate qualify me to join the mission agency that even had a base right there in my destination, the Ganges River area?

But the word of the Lord had come with crystal clarity. I was to go *now*, and I was to "live with the native people." Whatever might become of me, this constituted the first step on my mission. Unfortunate predecessors having attempted to "live with the native people" in other exotic lands had been speared to death. I could only close my eyes and go forward, trusting that my path wouldn't terminate in oblivion.

So a few days before my departure, partly out of faith and partly out of trepidation, I had waited for a time when Mom was outside and Dad was sleeping. Extracting a sheet of paper, I wrote a letter that read thusly:

Dear Mom and Dad,
  Thank you for being the best parents in the world. You've supported me and encouraged me in everything.

Now, as I depart to India, I believe God will protect me. But in case I don't return, don't worry or grieve too much because I'm with Jesus and we'll meet someday in heaven.

I love you,
Leanna

Fitted in amongst the manila folders in the file cabinet was one that Mom accessed monthly—"Budgeting." Into it I slipped the rough-drawn "last will and testament," knowing she'd find it at the end of the month when she balanced the checkbook. Soon afterward, with money earned by being the fastest busser ever to clear a table at Tobies Restaurant, I bought a one-way ticket to Delhi.

With one last sloppy kiss, Dad reluctantly released my hand. Mom delivered one more hug and a "Go with God!" as I shouldered the mountaineering backpack she had redesigned to contain a bulky twenty-pound video projector, my strategy to make inroads to the villagers by showing a film.

The moment my sneaker crossed the threshold from jet bridge to 747, a sensation of complete abandon swept over me. My equestrian career was gone. The grand facility Dad built for me had been sold for barely the money we had invested, not to count Dad's five years of hard labor. Friends and counselors thought I was nuts. Now I was potentially bereaving my mother and dying father of their only offspring.

But I afforded access neither to selfishness nor sentiment. My propulsion was that of a warrior going out to battle. A threefold motivation compels the soldier to endanger his life: the safety and freedom of others, love for his country and respect for the general who goes beside him. Likewise in that season, emotion played no part nor gave origin to the urge, but rather a deep yearning, portentous of impending doom yet hopeful of victory. The foundation of my soul, like a creeping vine, had found its lattice and had anchored itself to an unseen mystery far ahead, the purpose for which I had been conceived. Now it pulled me there, and I was eager to follow into the unknown.

The great engines of the 747 roared and up we rose. From the window I watched the last rays of evening light fade into darkness as the plane nosed out across the Atlantic. It was happening. I was en route to the place of chains, the lair of the warlords. The real conquest was now under way.

4

In the Epicenter

"The people living in darkness have seen a great
light; on those living in the land of the shadow
of death a light has dawned."

Matthew 4:16

*T*he breeze in my face provided minute but welcome relief
from the scorching heat as I pedaled my cycle bouncily
over the dust-drunk ever-under-construction thoroughfare.
The entire surface of a typical Indian street is one continuous
minefield of potholes, and the roadsides crawl with hawkers
of everything from vegetables to bracelets to clothing. From
street dogs to children, every living creature is engaged in a
ceaseless struggle to eke out a living in a culture of austerity. Only the rats, romping about on garbage heaps, are fat,
carefree and frolicsome.

The vision of the anthill hadn't been an exaggeration. The Indian road is far less orderly than a stream of ants. At least the ants have one goal and travel back and forth between two distinct points. On the Indian road, for every two bodies traveling along it, another is meandering across it with no heed to what is coming, or is stationary in the middle of it, such as cows or broken-down lorries. On equal par with gas pedal, brakes and steering, a vehicle's noisemaker is essential. Without the horn, life and limb of anybody crossing the road or traveling along it does so at great peril. Between the incessant *ding-a-ling* of cycles, *brrrrring* of rickshaws, bantam *beep* of autos and scooters, ear-stabbing blasts of politicians' 1950s-model Ambassador cars and musical intonations of lorries, the Indian road is a physical and auditory madhouse, the epitome of minimally organized chaos.

All of which I had come to rather enjoy. The challenge of weaving in and out of traffic and racing boys who thought a girl couldn't ride a bike ignited my competitive juices. On the Indian road there are no rules except two: Rule number one is, "Don't hit anybody." But when you do hit somebody, which is inevitable, it usually amounts to nothing more traumatic than a bent cycle wheel, a bloody toe or elbow and an exchange of rotten looks.

Rule number two is, "Size matters." If you're riding a cycle or a motorbike and a bus is coming, you move way over onto the shoulder and keep an eye on that bus. If the bus happens to be passing a slow-moving vehicle, it may decide to occupy the entire remainder of the road, including the shoulder on your side, in which case you must be prepared to topple into the ditch!

Upon my arrival in India a few months before, my Beloved had shone a light on one passage in the book of Joshua. The verse read, "Every place that the sole of your foot shall tread upon, that have I given unto you" (1:3 KJV). That had been God's promise to Joshua, preparing him to lead the nation of Israel into the Promised Land. Now God had bestowed the same promise upon me. That which I already knew from the dreams and visions had been confirmed. I must place my feet on this land as a representative of my Beloved, as a bearer of His love and light. I had been commissioned to open the way to freedom for the ragged captives.

But how should I, in my weak humanity, liberate tens of thousands and millions upon millions of people enslaved to superstition and poverty and disease and slavery? The idea smacked of a dwarf undertaking to displace Mount Everest.

Only one consolation stood: I was not alone. Upon my shoulder rested the hand of my Beloved, Creator and Master of mountains. He had drafted me into His mission. I had been prepared and honed as a weapon in His arsenal, a tool in His hand, a means whereby His presence and authority must come to bear against the bulwarks of darkness.

Thus I trod forward, carrying out that which I knew and declining to concern myself with that which I didn't yet know. My immediate assignment involved breaking fallow ground, preparing the way for a greater liberation yet to come. I walked and prayed. Placed my feet on the dusty roads and narrow alleyways crisscrossing the city like five messed-up spiderwebs overlaid on themselves. While doing so, I declared, as a representative of the rightful King, the defeat of the dark powers holding the people in slavery and the dawning of a new era of spiritual and physical liberty, healing and prosperity over the land.

Now He had revealed my second assignment—to openly praise and exalt the true King on the steps of the *ghats*, the great stone stairways along the river where seekers solicited the attention and blessing of the only gods they knew. Upon arriving in India, I discovered several groups of believers, all of them either internationals like myself or Indians from the more evangelized and typically more civilized regions farther south. I supposed they would have already been engaging in this type of warfare, leveraging the authority of the true King against the powers of darkness. But when I related my agenda, the Christian leaders had declined participation. They indicated that open worship of Jesus along the Ganges would be a seriously unwise undertaking.

But what else could I do? My Beloved had spoken. His intentions were unmistakable.

Admittedly, it was a disquieting thought. How would the warlords respond when their enemy's ambassador stood on their doorstep lauding their enemy? Would the strongman easily give up the house he had occupied for millennia? No. It constituted a declaration of war. Over this very issue of worship in eons past, the warlords and their boss, Lucifer, and a third of the angelic armies had rebelled and were kicked out of heaven. These principalities of darkness reveled in the ceaseless veneration that ascended to them through prayers, bells, incense and offerings from the core of their stronghold on Planet Earth—the three-mile stretch of *ghats* bounding the mighty Ganges.

My cycle wheels churned up dust as I pedaled my way toward the concrete rooftop apartment where I lived with an Indian family, Vincent and Priti and their sons, Ruel and Josh. The rumblings in my stomach weren't sure if they were hunger pains or indigestion. Upon my arrival in India, my

Beloved had instructed me, *Live at the same standard as the Indians.* That meant I was not to use my $200-per-month income to buy much beyond that which was common to my host family. The type of bed they slept on, I was to sleep on, even though it consisted of a half-inch mat on a concrete floor in close comradery with resident mice, ants, lizards and cockroaches. The food the natives ate, I was to eat, and the water they drank, I was to drink.

Problem was, without a moment's hesitation the natives chugged down brown-tinted tap water or, when drawn from an open village well, yellow-tinged water with floaters. The imbibing of polluted water explained their frequent illnesses, but at that time in India water filters were rare and far beyond the average budget. One of my assignments had been to acclimate my digestive tract to the water. Thus I had now joined the Indians in enduring intermittent bouts of various maladies, including gas attacks, diarrhea, constipation, sinus infections and, trumping the troublesomeness of them all, nasty, excruciating, pus-oozing boils.

Meals consisted primarily of three substances: *suji* porridge for breakfast, *daal* lentil soup and rice for lunch and for supper, gooey gray-green eggplant and more *daal* sopped up with rice or flat bread called *roti.* Though nutritious, these comprised about the only items on the menu. After weeks of porridge, lentils and eggplant, I realized that Indian families consider themselves fortunate to be able to eat three meals a day. If those meals included protein and a bit of vegetables, they were content. Variety and taste was not of particular importance. Eating, I concluded, was not expected to induce pleasure but was undertaken out of necessity.

Yet at the same time, I knew the hard, cold reason why this precious family consumed primarily lentils and eggplant.

They couldn't afford tasty food. This was the standard lot of the vast majority of people in India. Meat, eggs and other delicacies, such as pastries and sweets and milk, barring a bit dribbled into the tea, were beyond their budget. To have such foods on a regular basis equated to a Western family dining daily in five-star restaurants on lobster tail and filet mignon—financially untenable.

But as the weeks dragged into months, try though I might to adapt, my ability to palate this relentless diet of carbs with a scant smattering of vegetables steadily decreased. Having for 26 years enjoyed the heartiness of American bounty, my system rebelled. The thought of more lentil mush and gooey eggplant elicited mental images of baby poop and cow snot. Thus, to Priti's cheerful "Dinner's ready!" I had begun to reply "Thanks, but I'm fasting today."

Then a redeeming fact dawned on me: "Today is Ruel's birthday!"

Indian families typically possess no ovens, and most can't afford a store-bought cake or presents. So for those on a tight income, birthdays tend to be overlooked. Even tender tots may pass their special day no differently than others, receiving but a fleeting "Happy birthday" and, if they're lucky, a ten-rupee off-brand candy bar from a nearby general store. But every family, given the means, loves to throw a party on their child's big day.

"Birthday! Reason to celebrate! *Meat for dinner!*"

No sooner had this tantalizing thought wafted into my mind than the handlebars of my cycle turned off on a side road toward the promising reek of chicken droppings, giblets and blood. Wheeling up to the rickety shed tacked together with rotten boards and tar paper, I assessed the options. Panting droopily, feathers broken and soiled from subsisting in a four-foot cage, eight miserable white fowl awaited their fate. Uncharacteristically rotund for a shopkeeper, the butcher stretched and stood from his cross-legged sprawl on a raised wood platform, which also served as chopping block. Neither he nor I cared that his clothes and face were spattered red from preparing his wares for the last ten customers, or that a plague-black swarm of flies blanketed the butcher block.

"How many kilograms?" he inquired in Hindi.

Swallowing the saliva that had already begun to anticipate the feast, I grinned. "Give me the biggest one you've got!"

The near-comatose birds emitted muffled clucks and squawks as he stuck his hand in the cage and groped about, feeling their breasts for meatiness. Then he nabbed one by the leg and dragged it out. The bird screeched and flapped desperately for the few seconds of its transport to the chopping block. With a sudden buzzing, the flies took wing, blackening the air. In three swift motions the butcher folded the cock's wings, placed its neck on the wood and lifted the cleaver.

Thunk. The head of Ruel's soon-to-be birthday dinner rolled onto the floor. The butcher chucked the quivering body into a bucket to bleed out.

The guts spilled out with a single twist of his hand, and after salvaging heart and liver, were flung—*splat*—into a pile at the back of the hut. After ripping off the skin and feathers, the butcher's feet went into gear. Seated on the platform with the handle of a small super-sharp blade gripped between his toes, he sliced off the wings and thighs. Then, with a cleaver, he hacked the works into dainty pieces—the Indian strategy by which six people can be served two pieces of chicken each out of a scrawny bird not much meatier than a quail.

Into a black plastic bag plopped my bloody, warm chicken pieces, and then onto the metal pan of a balance scale. The

141

butcher lifted the fulcrum, placing a weight onto the opposing pan. The height of the two pans swayed to approximately equal. *"Ek kilogram, teen sau gram,"* he muttered.

Into the grimy hand of the butcher I placed 150 rupees, then concealed the black bag within my backpack lest our staunchly vegetarian landlord witness me entering the building with the telltale packaging employed exclusively by sellers of "non-veg."

"Happy birthday, Ruel!" I announced upon sliding the bolt of the creaky steel door behind me. A bloodcurdling scream emitted from the far room, and two Tasmanian devils hurtled down the hall. Ruel plowed into me, sprawled on the concrete floor and lay moaning, hoping I would believe him to be mortally wounded. Josh grabbed for the black bag, clamoring, "What did you bring? What did you bring?"

I raised it up out of his reach but produced a giant Cadbury chocolate bar procured on my way between chicken shack and home. No longer wounded, Ruel erupted off the floor and leaped, screaming, for the candy bar. Releasing it into Josh's hands, I ordered, "Share nicely with your brother."

The children successfully appeased, I headed for the kitchen. Hands full of *roti* dough, Priti took one look in the bag and gasped. "Chicken! You bought chicken! Thank you! This will be the best birthday ever!"

That evening when Vincent returned from his day of ministry sweaty, grimy from road dust and exhausted from battling traffic and preaching, he brought green vegetables offered by the villagers. So we enjoyed a sumptuous dinner of chicken curry, *roti* and greens with Priti's delectable spice preparation. Mom had instilled in me a commitment to non-wastage, especially when no dogs were present to scarf the scraps, but watching the Indians devour that chicken redefined gratitude and austerity. They chewed the chicken bones right down to nothing, enjoying this treat to the uttermost molecule of marrow and cartilage, until nothing remained on their plates but dry splinters.

Stomach adequately appeased, my thoughts returned to the task ahead. Tomorrow would be the big day. My search for people to accompany me was over. Now it was just me and my Beloved aiming a beam of His authority at the root of the chains binding the nation in slavery and darkness. Whatever the consequences, I knew this was my immediate assignment. Whatever the outcome, I would not put it off a day longer. The time to officially engage the warlords on their own turf had arrived.

Well before the searing sun had risen enough to enflame the southeast-facing riverbank in scorching heat, I swung off my cycle, chained it to a pole and stood at the top of one of the highest *ghats*.

Gazing down at the bustling humanity below and the wide floodplain beyond, another wave of *"This is crazy"* hit me. Once I ventured down there and began my song, what did I propose to answer if anyone asked what I was doing? Despite my fervent study of Hindi prior to my embarkation to India, my first few attempts to converse had proven my inability to speak a single intelligible sentence. Nor could I understand the stream of impossibly fast, jumbled gibberish that tumbled from the lips of the natives and bore not an iota of similarity to the voice on my *Teach Yourself Hindi* cassette. My solace entailed having memorized the Hindi script, enabling me to read . . . at the halting speed of a first grader. By following along in the songbook when I sat in prayer groups, I had managed to learn a few worship choruses.

So here I was, with my arsenal of five songs, but no ability whatsoever to explain my presence to the friendly inquisitive, much less to hostile inquisitors.

Guitar bobbing on my back and stack of Gospel booklets in a plastic bag, I breathed a prayer and descended from the temples and guesthouses about halfway to the river below. There I seated myself on a great flagstone step, unzipped the canvas guitar cover and began to play and sing. The lyrics carried a clear message of Jesus' love, sacrifice and resurrection.

Within minutes two beggar children trudged by bearing tin cans and bits of magnet tied on a string, utilized for gleaning coins offered to the river goddess. Noticing me, they turned aside hoping to gain a rupee and stood staring as do children who haven't been taught etiquette. I smiled at them and continued my song.

A young man who had been trying to persuade customers to rent his boat joined the children, staring likewise, but with a suspicious scowl. After him came two ladies on their way to offer flowers to the river, and then others clustered around, attracted by the crowd, from toothless old men swathed in Gandhi-style *dhotis* to bright-faced middle-class children with their kites or cricket bats. Soon I was overshadowed by a sea of faces, questioning, wondering, curious and a few disapproving. My audience listened attentively to the songs, and in between some spoke up in Hindi.

"Who is Jesus?" an old man muttered.

Another queried, "You purport that Jesus was God among us and He died for our sin and then came back to life? I've never heard of a God who overcame death."

To which another rejoined, "But Lord Krishna was god on earth."

The former replied, "But Krishna didn't die for our sin and rise from the dead."

The chattering died down the moment I strummed another song. Still incapable of making proper conversation in Hindi, I didn't attempt to talk with the people. Instead, when I tired of singing or ran out of tunes, I handed them Gospel booklets, which they received with exuberance. Schoolchildren paired up with friends and the illiterate elderly joined them to hear the booklet read aloud.

Contrary to the fearful warnings, the people had proved warmly receptive. Several weeks passed and my confidence grew. I positioned myself at different spots along the *ghats* and repeated this "invasion." My assignment from my Beloved wasn't so much to directly influence the people. It was to make a declaration against the minions, asserting the presence and authority of the true King, Jesus, in the face of those spiritual principalities that held the land and the people in bondage.

But one day when I sat down and began my strumming and singing, the people declined to gather around. They stood far off, down by the river's edge, watching intently. Why did they keep such a distance? Something was wrong, but what?

My puzzlement would be short-lived. While mulling over these observations, I sensed a presence. Looking up from my guitar, I choked on my breath at what bore down on me.

A few yards to my right stood a hut barely three feet wide, decorated with gold-fringed red flags and wooden beads of multiple shapes. A special retreat set up for a special purpose.

From within this private ashram a figure moved—a human form, but at the same time not human. From the darkness emerged a being of such death-like terror he might as well have stepped off the TV screen from a zombie flick. He was entirely nude excepting a scant loincloth and lavish garlands of beads around his neck. Instead of the usual brown of the Indian skin, his emaciated body was a mottled whitish-gray, smeared and caked with cremation ash. Matted and twining about themselves, a mass of dreadlocks were partly mounded on top of his head, the rest descending past his buttocks. White and red paint streaked his forehead, and his fist clenched a marigold-swathed steel trident, the weapon of the warlord prince called Destroyer.

Bone-chilling beyond his bodily attire or lack thereof were his eyes—pits of blackness, sunken and dead. They were whirlpools, pulling, sucking, draining life from whatever they latched on to, like the teeth of a vampire. His eyes reached out, ravenous and at the same time enslaved. This was a human being whom God loved. But unlike others who were bound by the chains that swooped down from the hands of the warlords, this man had given himself over completely to darkness. He had become their executor. The warlords looked out through the eyes of their slave. They'd had enough of me, and now it was showdown time.

Far down by the riverbank, the people knew exactly what was going on. The foolhardy foreigner, they mused, had chosen the wrong place to sit and thus had raised a brazen challenge to their gods. Now they waited to see who could prove preeminence.

The match was on—the warlords versus Jesus.

Trident raised, the fearsome persona strode toward me fixated, neither looking right nor left. The ash on his body cracked. His bare feet flapped on the stone steps. His lips moved, and I knew he was uttering incantations and spells against me.

What would happen when he reached me?

A flood of the presence of my Beloved surged through me with an unseen bolt of lightning from above, and my eyes locked with those gleaming whirlpools to hell. For a split second we were, in the spirit realm, two wrestlers grappling for takedown.

My mouth opened and I began proclaiming the name of the One who had triumphed over demonic power, the name at the sound of which hell trembles and heaven shouts, the name of the One who had defeated the enemy of creation . . . the name of the Holy One, the greatest Treasure, whose sacrifice had liberated the universe. The chorus I sang directly into the face and injected into the eyes of the advancing high priest of darkness was the Hindi version of this:

> There is power, power, wonder-working power in the
> blood of the Lamb.
> There is power, power, wonder-working power in the
> precious blood of the Lamb.

With scarcely three paces remaining between us, the witch doctor stopped. He froze, as motionless as the stone images nearby. Even his lips suspended in the middle of a phrase, brown teeth parted, breathing abated. The invading darkness of his eyes melted. His pupils dilated, and his eyelids raised wide in terror. In a matter of seconds what had been a fiend on the attack transformed into a frail old man who had seen a ghost . . . or my guardian angel.

Then, swift as a private under the command of a general, he about-faced and fled back into the ashram.

Hardly did I have time to comprehend what had happened, before a tumult of shouting voices and running feet jerked my gaze toward the river. A wall of people stampeded

147

toward me, and before I knew what was happening, a tangle of brown arms grabbed the plastic bag of Gospel booklets and ripped it open.

They were shouting in Hindi, "Jesus defeated our most powerful guru. Jesus is the true Lord, the living God!"

The people were desperate to know the God who had overpowered the witch doctor. Figuring the foreigner was incapable of a coherent discourse in Hindi, they craved my booklets, which they knew contained the answer they sought. Booklets flew everywhere as the people dove for them, and when the supply was exhausted, they grappled one another for possession.

That day people who were chained in generations of superstition and fear saw that there is One greater who can give them life and liberty. For a fleeting moment, "the people who walked in darkness" had glimpsed the mystery and the treasure that is Jesus (Matthew 4:16).

My first assignment had involved treading the length and breadth of this city, the mecca of spiritual oppression over the nation. Wherever I walked, I declared through word and presence that the powers gripping the chains of bondage were trespassers on this land.

Now this latest season had also come to a close as Mystery led me on, one step at a time, with nothing but void beyond.

Yet a final act of spiritual chain–breaking remained before the season would change. This step would be yet more audacious, taking me into the very epicenter of the warlords' stronghold.

Along with my current jobs of hacking away at the spiritual dimension through prayer and spiritual warfare, I assumed that eventually I would learn Hindi well enough to follow the path of so many before—preaching and telling the people about Jesus. I could only hope that I would score greater success than others.

But Mystery would route me on a wholly different course. My Beloved had purposely steered me away from the traditional methods and joined me as one with the native people. The strategy He was about to reveal would not lead to sooty coal mines of traditional methods but to caverns shimmering with unspeakable treasure—treasure encased in cold, cruel darkness, waiting to be set free to fulfill the shining destiny for which it had been created.

Buffalo-Tipping in the Ganges

One by one the auto rickshaws arrived. Their two-stroke engines sputtered, coughed and died as they drew up at the appointed rendezvous—a popular tea stall near the highway. Situated at the northeast edge of the city, it was the safest place in this urban area from which to carry out our dangerous mission.

A thin fog lingered over the river, cloaking its pollution, a piece of cotton tenderly placed on a wound. The steel doors of roadside shops were still locked down, and the streets were fairly quiet excepting an occasional cave-dim *dhaba* where jolly men fried sweet pastries in cauldrons of smoking oil and unbathed boys poured tea into thick-walled glasses hastily rinsed out from serving the previous customer.

The morning air was tangible with dust and smoke accented by an occasional waft of freshly fried *puri* bread, incense smoldering before idols and the rotting remains of a street dog putrefying along with watery garbage in the gutter. Pulsing across the ramshackle buildings from a nearby temple, *pooja* music exalted Krishna, Shiva and Durga through a brassy loudspeaker, while from another direction a summons to venerate Allah bugled from a *masjid*'s minaret. Barefoot women swathed in gaily hued *saris* and toting handbags bulging with offerings and a change of clothes made their way solemnly toward the river for their ritual bath and devotions to the rising sun and goddess Mother Ganges.

The Indian family that had accepted me as their own daughter had risen before dawn in preparation for this day. Priti had made Vincent and me a quick breakfast of chai and *sooji* porridge while shouting reprimands at Josh and Ruel. The appeal of a one-armed plastic Spider-Man and a toy truck without wheels far exceeded that of donning school uniforms.

"What will you do if the *gundas* come?" Priti glanced worriedly at her husband while prying Spider-Man from a screaming Ruel's fingers and stuffing his hand into a spiffy white sleeve.

Vincent shrugged. "Talk to them. Persuade them to leave us alone."

"If they won't leave you alone, then what?"

"*Aaray baba!* Please, honey, stop worrying!" he muttered into the dregs of his tea.

"What about Jyoti?" Priti persisted. "If the *gundas* see a foreigner with you, they'll give you terrible trouble."

Vincent stood, patted his wife reassuringly on the shoulder and donned his bill cap. "JD and Munulal are coming to help us, too. We'll be fine."

My backpack jammed with towels, clothes and a Bible, we set out. Starting the old Bullet bike always afforded Vincent a workout. By the twentieth kick, when it at last roared to life, he was sweating and the sky was becoming pink and

orange in the east. I climbed on behind and we thundered off
through trash-littered streets, swerving to miss the frequent
mangy street dog, meandering cow and broken blacktop.

At the tea stall we greeted our troop—JD and Munulal, the
first to follow Christ from this unreached region, their radiant faces testimony to the treasure they'd discovered. With
them, the new disciples led to Christ recently through our
village outreaches—timid village women smiling sheepishly,
faces half-covered with their *saris*, a wizened grandpa with
broken glasses taped together in the middle, a middle-aged
man whose persona attested to a degree of education and
status and a spry young husband and wife whose affinity for
one another, though mitigated by cultural boundaries, was
generously evident.

"*Jai masih ki, jai masih ki!*" Vincent and I moved among
the disciples shaking hands and embracing. Beaming faces
and exuberant joy rippled through the group, tempered by
the grave potential of opposition to what we were preparing to do.

"Everybody ready?" Vincent inquired of the eager faces.
Everyone fell mute and jovial smiles straightened.

The middle-aged man spoke for the rest: "Yes, we're ready."

"Let's go!"

We set off toward the river, calloused feet in blue flip-flops
and leather toe-loop sandals negotiating gutters and narrow alleyways. Children played in the doorways of tiny dark
hovels, and men on cycles squeezed past lumbering Brahma
bulls. Hawkers pushed carts laden with lush vegetables and
seasonal fruits, their mechanical voices contorted by over-
use, shouting out their wares for the women to come and
buy. Starkly contrasted against the faded, blackened greenish
paint of her home, a lady in a bright blue and yellow *sari*

held a pail into which a man dispensed fresh buffalo milk from one of four steel cans fastened by hooks alongside his worn cycle.

Leaving behind the temples and shops and streets and the bustling activity of the waking-up city, we trundled along above the river's edge until rickety homes and shops and pavement gave way to sandy dirt and shrubs and a clear view of the river below.

"Looks like a good place," observed Vincent.

"I'll go test the bottom," I offered.

"Stay here," Vincent admonished the group. "We'll go down and see if this is a good spot."

I was already off, bounding down the slope toward the river's edge. But with a few yards remaining between myself and the water, my pace slowed.

Something was wrong.

Bobbing up and down with the ebb and flow of the water was the usual pollution found in the Ganges—foamy bubbles produced by everything that happened upstream, including sewage outlets, ritual bathing and hotel chambermen washing laundry. Along with the foam, a few articles had run aground. Ceremonially immersed in the water as an offering to the river goddess, an idol's one remaining eye stared emptily from beneath a discarded Lay's potato chip bag, its wooden body swathed in mud-drenched red and gold sparkly cloth and decaying garlands of marigolds.

But something else had also washed up on this shore—a glob of matter that topped out as the most loathsome and revolting sight I had ever in my life beheld. One in motion with the foam and the idol and the marigolds, bloated and decayed beyond recognition, floated a human corpse.

"Aaray baba!" Vincent had come down the bank to see why I had frozen in place. Encountering the sight and stench, his mustache twitched with aversion. Not far upstream was the mortuary of India. Families transported their deceased multiple miles, believing that if the funeral pyre could be lit by the eternal flame and the ashes placed into the waters of holy Mother Ganges, the soul of the deceased would escape purgatory and possibly attain heaven.

Weekly I traversed the dismal ash-and-soot-encased haunt, interceding for the people and asserting the victory of Jesus' resurrection in the presence of the spiritual warlords stationed there. Around the funeral pyres clustered precious souls with fear in their eyes and despair on their faces—people whom God had created and loved, waiting to be liberated from the chains binding those who are yet to know that Jesus alone can give us eternal life.

"Floater break loose from rock," muttered Vincent. *"Chalo,* we go different place."

For once appreciative of the otherwise troublesome *dupatta* scarf, I clamped it over nose and mouth, its polyester threads offering scant relief from the overwhelming stench. Through the scarf I croaked, "What's a floater?"

While retracing our steps back up the bank, Vincent explained, "Some types of dead body they no burn them. Pregnant woman, baby, Hindu priest, leper. Those put out in middle of Ganges and tie rock on them. Sometimes they breaks loose from rock and come up on top of water. That is floater."

A brief conference ensued in Hindi between Vincent, JD and Munulal to decide what to do next. We had chosen this spot because of its remote location, away from potential opposition. To carry out our plans much closer to the temples would exponentially increase the danger of attracting unhealthy attention, potentially culminating in our being attacked with sticks, rocks and fists.

"One place is there upstream from dead body before temples," Munulal noted. "We try it?"

Everyone agreed, so off we trooped back the way we'd come, traveling closer to the river's edge to watch for the location. Treacherous rocks populating the silty shoreline intensified into sharp boulders. Around, over and between the rocks, their hooves churning the shoreline into a stinking quagmire, a sea of ponderous black bodies plodded and paddled both in and out of the water.

Buffalo.

They had no intention of moving. This was their daily bathing spot, the mud and water affording their enormous bodies blissful relief from the heat.

We drew up and gazed at the unpleasant sight. The only place we could possibly carry out our plans would be amidst the beasts and boulders, in thick, slimy water that consisted of some ratio of H_2O amalgamated with muddy buffalo dung.

"*Aaray babAAA!*" Vincent's mustache twitched, indicating he wasn't sure which was worse, the corpse water or the buffalo water.

JD waded out into the soup amidst the rocks, hands outstretched, knowing he was likely to fall since his poor eyesight prevented him from seeing much detail. The brown sludge soaked up his pant legs and splashed brownish-green onto his white shirt. One step, two, three . . .

Then he tripped on a submerged boulder and sprawled forward in a belly-*splat*, scaring three buffalo, which splashed off in different directions. He surfaced completely drenched

154

and laughing, pushed out farther. "Come on, it's fine!" he shouted.

Vincent sighed and cast a glance around for potential opposition. From upstream a rhythmic *slap . . . slap* indicated the presence of washermen beating laundry on rocks, then laying it out on the ground to dry. Some fifty yards distant a troop of schoolboys were intent on a game of cricket. Otherwise the coast looked clear.

"Okay, let's do it." Vincent waded into the water, and Munulal and I used our feet to feel out a minimally hazardous route. Then we guided the new believers in, holding the arms of the elderly to stabilize them. Soon we were up to our chests in the murky soup with the new believers lined up in single file.

At last the joyous event could finally begin—the ceremony that in India officially marks a person's choice to follow Jesus, and which therefore incites violent opposition from anti-Christians—baptism.

Bracing their feet precariously on the rocky river bottom, Vincent and JD positioned themselves on either side of the first new believer. I recognized her as Isha Devi, the lady who had been barren and tormented by debilitating stomach pain for years.

Isha's liberation from her chain of bondage happened several months earlier on one of those days when nothing was going right. Ashis's uncle Prasad had invited us to show the film in his village fifteen kilometers from the city. But on this day, after the twentieth kick, the Bullet still wouldn't start. By the thirtieth, Vincent was becoming exhausted, and at last he made a phone call, hoping desperately to reach Munulal. After persuading his brother to let him borrow the family's puttering Hero Poke scooter, he had come to the rescue.

Hauling the video equipment on Vincent's motorcycle was challenging enough, but fitting it onto the tiny scooter was going to constitute a circus act. Munulal planted his tailbone as far forward on the seat as possible, and Vincent hefted the sixty-pound generator on behind him. I piled the amp, stabilizer and VCR on top of the generator, along with a bag stuffed with two bedsheets sewn together for a screen, rope to suspend it from trees and power cords stacked on top of that. With the twenty-pound video projector in its pack on my back, I then squeezed my buttocks onto the few inches of black vinyl seat that remained and wrapped my arms over and around the generator.

Hitting bottom at every bump, we set out with the scooter engine screaming and Munulal calling upon every iota of his skill to balance. My grip on the generator served two essential purposes—to keep it and everything on top from pitching sideways, and to counterbalance me. The weight of the projector in my backpack and the lack of support beneath my hiney made each bounce and bump threaten to topple me off backward.

No road led to the village. Reaching the spot at which we must turn off the narrow strip of blacktop, Munulal brought the scooter to a jostling halt and gazed at the options ahead. Either we would have to negotiate a twelve-inch-wide raised dirt path intended for pedestrians and cycles, or else drive through a ploughed field. Balancing this load on the narrow path being obviously impossible, the ploughed field it must be. So the final leg of the journey, both hair-raising and exhilarating, taxed our balancing skills to the limit. We bounced and bumped and swerved through the field, but at last sputtered into the village.

Prasad and his wife and daughters-in-law and grandma and grandpa heeled by a gaggle of shy, giggling children, welcomed us with gusto. Self-conscious of their rotting teeth, the elders damped their smiles or covered their mouths with a bit of cloth while the younger ones wonderingly caressed my hands. Abandoning me to the women, Munulal and Prasad disappeared to set up the equipment. I was ushered into the molded mud-and-thatch hut to partake of the essential element of Indian hospitality—a cup of chai. Their innocent faces, some wizened beyond their years, others young and soft, searched mine, wondering, questioning, as if I were an alien from another planet.

During the raucous scooter ride, I had forgotten about my *dupatta*, which now dragged on the ground. One of the women gently restored it to its proper drape across my bosom. Another fixed my hair, and another brushed field dirt off the leg of my *salwar*. I courteously tolerated the coddling. The bolder ones tried to converse with me in the only language they knew—their village dialect. Having only begun to learn a bit of Hindi, I could not understand a word. When I ventured a few Hindi sentences of my own, their puzzled expressions and lack of response reiterated the excruciating fact that my pronunciation errors still rendered me unintelligible. One by one they gave up and sauntered back to the only other room in the hut—the tiny, dark, smoke-filled kitchen. I felt at once both ashamed and relieved. These beautiful people were so inquisitive and eager to hear even the simplest word I might communicate, yet I was helpless as a dumb jackass to do so.

The children remained nearby, timidly gazing at me from darting black eyes, then looking away giggling, jostling and piling half on top of their comrades. One boy with tousled hair ripped strips from a piece of sugarcane with brown-tinged teeth, chewed and sucked out the sweetness, then spat the pulp across the room.

"Come here." I reached a hand toward him. He stopped in mid-chew, grinned and flung the remainder of the cane stalk at his buddy. "Give me your hand." The boy stood and stuck out his right hand. I curled his grimy, sticky fingers around mine and raised my thumb, indicating for him to do likewise. *"Angutha larai."* I gave him a mischievous smirk. "Means 'thumb war.'" After a few seconds of dueling, I pinned his thumb and the increasingly attentive audience shouted and wide smiles spread across faces. Within minutes they had caught on. Thumb Wrestle Mania swept from the hut out into the packed-mud yard, as kids ran and shouted and challenged one another, then insisted that the adults stop their work and watch. The smiles passed to the women, who now looked at me differently. This facile icebreaker transformed me from alien to human.

Outside, dusk had closed in, which meant it was time to set up for the show. But in the distance I could hear an unwelcome sound—the generator cord being pulled over and over without so much as a sputter of life. The bouncy ride had sogged the spark plug, I figured, and Munulal hadn't thought to take it out and dry it off.

Trailed and tugged on by laughing children, I made my way past cud-chewing, balloon-bellied buffalo tethered to posts in the ground and playful goats wagging their heads at passersby with hope of provoking them to a butting match. Figuring out where I was headed, the children trotted ahead and led out on the narrow packed-dirt pathways between the fields.

"Did you take out the spark plug?" I inquired.

The youth released the starter cord and stared at me, wiping sweat from his brow. "Please repeat?"

I sighed. Great; even he didn't understand my Hindi. I snapped the cover off the spark plug and tried to unscrew it.

"*Ho gaya plug nikal kar chukha,*" protested Munulal. "*Abhi start nahi ho paya.*" That meant he had already tried drying off the spark plug and it hadn't worked.

I straightened, now suspecting the cause of the dead generator to be spiritual warfare. The difficulty of starting the generator posed a regular challenge to showing the film, but usually the spark plug was the solution. "Pray," I instructed Munulal. "We'll try again later."

Upon hitting what appears to be an immovable roadblock, my nature is to leave it and make progress in other areas, then come back to the roadblock again, knowing that striving isn't the answer and that the Lord would make a way. Observing that none of the other equipment had been prepared, I suggested we proceed by faith to set up the rest of the show.

Two boys hauled a wooden bed out of a hut, on which I arranged the projector, stabilizer, VCR and amplifier. Munulal and Prasad assayed to hang the sheet between a tree and a bamboo pole protruding from the unfinished brick wall of a neighbor's hut. Assisted by an exuberant youth who gripped the tree with his bare feet and propelled himself straight up the limbless trunk to bind the rope, the fifteen-foot sheet was now the ready backdrop for an outdoor theater. The audience of gawking, chattering villagers grew, since our efforts constituted the sole excitement having taken place here for longer than they could remember.

Hiring of the speakers having been prearranged by Vincent, two youths arrived across a field carrying two black boxes, and fixed the wires into the back of the amp. Then a welcome sound, still distant but nonetheless distinct, hammered through the airwaves—Vincent's Bullet.

Praise God, it started, I thought. *Maybe he'll know what's wrong with the generator.* I stuck the power cord into the projector and commenced to plug the other end into the power strip, only to discover that my U.S.-to-Indian adapter was gone. A desperate search ensued, me pawing through the remaining cords in the bag and searching the smallest pockets of the backpack while Munulal retraced our steps from the scooter.

No adapter.

"No worry, we will make village connection." Vincent had arrived and watched our frenzy with his usual nonchalance, dipping a biscuit into the cup of tea dutifully offered by a fully veiled woman whom I would later learn was Isha Devi. He motioned to the youths who had finished connecting the amp and speakers, then inspected the generator.

Munulal poured out the story of its uncooperativeness and his endless, exhausting attempts to start it.

"Did you pray?" Vincent inquired, smiling.

"Ha ji, prathna kiya bhaya." Yes, Munulal had prayed.

"Okay, then start it!"

With a sigh, Munulal grasped the starter cord again and gave it a pull. No life. But with the second crank, the generator purred to life. The audience of villagers clapped and cheered. Now confident they would get to enjoy a movie, those watching from doorways ducked inside and elders standing around the generator shooed the youngsters off on mission. Village homes lack chairs, and it's uncouth to sit directly on the bare earth where a residue of garbage, spittle or feces occupies every square foot. The children swiftly reappeared toting rags or gunnysacks or pieces of plastic, any substance to place between their bottoms and the ground.

The generator had warmed up, and we began to breathe easier, confident that it wasn't going to quit. I turned back to the projector, and there a sight awaited me that would strike terror into anyone having responsibility for a fragile $3,000 piece of high-tech electronics. "Village connection" meant the boys had wrapped bare wire around the two pins of my projector plug and jammed the other ends of the wire into the power strip.

"What if something touches those wires? Won't it short-circuit my projector?" I attempted to ask in Hindi. They didn't understand me, and I decided it wasn't worthwhile to pursue the issue further. Tonight the projector would be connected the "village way" or not at all, and I resolved to stand guard over that connection to ensure no unruly child or wandering goat tripped over it in the dark.

So with no further hiccups, the program commenced. A single bulb affixed to our power board emitted sufficient light for us to accomplish our work, but meanwhile it attracted a ravenous swarm of winged insects, which crawled into my hair, attempted to fly up my nostrils and found their way inside my dress and down my bra. With every eye in the village on me, extracting them at that moment was unthinkable.

Munulal took the microphone, and with volume sufficient for the whole village to hear, announced in the village dialect that the movie was soon to start. He told them it was about *Yeshu Masih* and that through Him people could be set free from fear and sickness and demonic bondage because *Yeshu Masih* had overcome sin and death. Sandals slapping hard-packed mud and scuffing along narrow pathways between huts, upright forms silhouetted against beige walls arrived, and soon a sea of humanity filled the narrow grounds. Others climbed up on rooftops or pulled aside the tarp covering glassless windows or sat in their doorsteps to watch from a distance.

Then it was showtime. With a prayer that the generator would keep running, that the VHS hadn't collected too much dust and that the precarious wiring connecting the projector to the power would carry the voltage, I pressed the button that turned on the lamp. The purring generator lugged down, coughed, then chugged into work mode as the 1,000-lumen LCD beamed "Epson" onto the sheet. Munulal, in training to run the VCR, pressed Play and the movie began.

The usual order of business was to switch off the light bulb the moment everything was running to reduce the load on the generator, and tonight I was especially thankful when our table was swathed in darkness and all eyes were fixed ahead on the screen. I could now dare to fish the six-legged critters out of my underwear, scratch the itches they had aroused and relax. Isha, her face still concealed by her *sari*, served us a second cup of chai and biscuits while the villagers settled in and imbibed with rapt fascination a Bollywood-style depiction of the birth, life, crucifixion and resurrection of Jesus.

When the movie ended, we switched the bulb on, and for extra light, left the projector lamp on, too. Vincent took the mic and explained in Hindi that Jesus was the one true and living God and that anyone following Him must stop worshiping other gods and idols. "Jesus alone can give you *moksh*—liberation and eternal life—because He suffered the penalty for our sin and then rose again. He won the victory over death and the devil.

"But," Vincent warned, "if you're ready to receive Jesus' gift of salvation tonight, it will cost you. People will persecute you. Your family may throw you out, mock you and even beat you. So take time now and decide: Will you follow Jesus . . . no matter what the cost?"

A long moment of stillness followed. The villagers stood with bowed heads. Even the children who had begun to fidget and scamper here and there hushed.

Vincent looked around at them. "Okay. Are you ready?" A few heads nodded. "Who is ready to follow Jesus?" Some ten hands raised, faces serious and somber, but eager with anticipation.

"Thank You, Lord," Vincent murmured aside from the mic. Then addressing the people again, "Pray after me." He led them in a prayer, confessing their sin to God, receiving Jesus' forgiveness and committing their lives to serving Him.

"Amen. . . . Now, if you prayed from your heart, then this day you begin new life! God's love and power is living inside you. Let's rejoice!" Munulal took the mic and led into a rousing praise song in the local village "Bhajan" style. The people joined in with clapping, and a man and two ladies began to dance, sobriety replaced by celebration.

After the song, Munulal invited anyone who was sick to come and receive prayer.

Among those who came forward was Isha Devi. She was the young wife of Munulal's cousin Ramesh, and since their marriage over a year ago, she had been unable to conceive and had suffered continuous abdominal pain.

Prasad related their plight. "We take her to witch doctor and hospital and temple and mosque, but she get worse and worse. Now our money gone and we lose our hope," he cried.

"Can she remove her veil?" asked Vincent.

"She is youngest daughter-in-law in family, so she wear veil," explained Munulal.

"Fine, but for now, can we see her face?"

Isha slipped the veil back enough to reveal the edge of her smooth black, well-oiled hair, silvery in the hard light of the projector and bulb. She gazed up at Vincent with a mixture of fear and hopelessness. Marring the beauty of her chiseled face was a red bruise, crescent-shaped, below her right eye.

"What happen here?" queried Vincent.

Prasad squirmed and stared at his feet.

"Ramesh get angry sometimes," admitted Munulal. "It shame for family if woman can't have baby."

Controlling the anger that seethed up in him, Vincent blew out his breath and ran a hand through his hair. "Where's Ramesh?" he demanded.

Munulal darted off and returned towing a young man bearing the expression of a cornered rabbit. The audience pressed in to see what would happen.

Vincent leveled his finger in Ramesh's face. "You see this woman? Is this your wife?"

Ramesh's eyes were riveted to his feet. "Yes, sir," he muttered.

"You must love and care for wife, and no harsh with her. Understood?"

"Yes, sir. I'm sorry I lost my temper." Ramesh tried to shrink into the ground.

"Do you drink?"

"A little."

"Stop it."

"Yes, sir, I know it's bad habit."

Vincent softened and lowered his voice. "It's good that you want to change, but you need God's help. Did you watch the movie?"

"Yes, sir."

"Do you know what Holy Bible says about marriage?"

The shame in Ramesh's eyes shifted to a willingness to learn. "No, sir, tell me."

Knowing the routine, I rummaged in Vincent's backpack and procured his Hindi Bible before he could ask for it. He found the passage, handed the Bible to Ramesh and pointed. "Read."

Ramesh read aloud, "Husbands . . . love your wives as . . . Christ also loved . . . the Church . . . and gave Himself . . . for her."

"Very good. God alone can enable you to love your wife like Jesus loves. Did you confess your sin and commit to follow Jesus when we prayed?"

"Yes." Now Ramesh's eyes gazed straight into Vincent's. "I believe in Jesus, and I want to change. I want to be good husband."

Vincent smiled and slapped him on the back. "*Shabash!* Excellent! Now . . ." He turned to Isha. "Do you believe Jesus can heal your stomach and give you a child?"

Watching the transformation in her husband, Isha had brightened considerably. "Yes, I believe."

Munulal and I drew near while Vincent placed Ramesh's hand on his wife's shoulder and instructed, "God's Spirit gives the power to heal, and He flows through believers. So join us and let's pray for your wife." The men laid their hands on Isha's shoulders and I placed mine on her abdomen. Munulal prayed in his native dialect and then Vincent prayed in Hindi and I prayed in English.

Isha looked around startled and exclaimed, "The pain in my stomach . . . is gone!"

"Since how long back you have pain?" asked Vincent.

"Since I was girl—since thirteen year."

"Now all gone?"

Isha was beaming. "Yes, no pain. Gone."

The villagers standing around murmured, "Jesus can heal! Jesus is the true Lord."

Ramesh embraced Isha even though Indian culture deems such behavior inappropriate in public, and began to shout, "Thank You, Jesus!"

Not long after that night, we received word that Ramesh and Isha now enjoyed a harmonious marriage. What was more, God had opened her womb, and she was a proud and contented expectant mother.

In Hindi Vincent proclaimed, "I baptize you in the name of the Father, and the Son, and the Holy Spirit."

With that, he and JD dipped Isha backward under the brown-green water and brought her up again. The sparkle of the morning sun in the droplets falling from her face accented the radiance of her smile. Today she made public confession of her new life in Jesus, the One who had died and risen again to liberate her from the chains of sin, disease and barrenness. Behind her, waiting his turn, stood Ramesh, delivered from the chains of alcoholism and committed to being a loving husband and soon-to-be father.

In the joy and glory of the moment, we would have forgotten the filth of the water and the goosh oozing up between our toes and the danger of persecution, if it hadn't been for the buffalo.

Water buffalo can be menacing critters, known to charge a stranger who encroaches their personal space. But they also have a curious streak, and today they were supremely inquisitive as to why a bunch of silly humans would crash their bathing party. When Ramesh waded forward to be baptized, a buffalo also approached, brown water lapping over its back, hooves barely touching bottom, half-floating like a giant black balloon.

"Go!" Vincent shouted and waved his arm, but the hairy head with beady little eyes and wagging ears and quivering nostrils kept on coming. In another split second, it would blunder right over Vincent and Ramesh. At the risk of slipping under the putrid water, Munulal lunged at the buffalo, flailing his arms and yelling. The buffalo turned aside.

After Ramesh had been dunked, he, Munulal and I arrayed ourselves in a protective triangle around Vincent, JD and the other believers. When a buffalo tried to enter our demarcated space, one of us gave its neck a shove, whereupon the half-floating beast emitted a startled bellow, toppled sideways, then scramble-paddled off in a different direction.

The delight of celebrating new lives rescued from darkness mingled with hysterical laughter, rendering truly unforgettable the day of buffalo-tipping in the Ganges.

My Beloved had promised, *Every place that the sole of your foot shall tread upon, that have I given unto you.* In response, I had now traversed practically every narrow alleyway of pavement and cobblestone within the stronghold city, and had proclaimed the rightful King up and down the length of the warlords' doorstep. Now the time had come to execute the third and final act in the process of tilling spiritual sod, a preparation for greater liberations to come.

There was one strategic location in which I had not yet tilled the sod: the temples.

Having faced down the naked witch doctor, I proceeded without hesitation to carry out this new assignment. By masquerading as a geography student at the local university, I had persuaded the Survey of India office to sell me a four-foot square map that contained the minute details of the city, including the locations of temples and names of roads. My daily activity involved identifying another temple, finding my way there and informing the presiding spiritual powers that they were trespassers and that the people they held captive were to be freed.

At last there remained only one major temple where I hadn't gone—the epicenter, the Kaaba of India, pilgrimage destination of millions. Tradition held that the pool of water beneath the ancient temple's gold-plated dome constituted the very fluid from which the universe had come into being. The people believed it had the power to atone for some of their sins and thus to afford the worshiper a vague possibility of direct entrance into heaven, or at least a shorter duration of torment in the terrifying hands of the gods and demons. This, along with other legends and religious rituals, constituted a heart-wrenching counterfeit, a spurious forgery of the blood of Jesus, which alone can reunite sinful humans with a holy God. It served as a placebo, placating the poor in the assumption that misery, poverty and sickness was their inescapable destiny until death swept them into oblivion.

The epicenter was last for a reason; it formed the warlords' citadel, root of the spiritual chains over the land. Militarily speaking, I had so far only bantered with the peons, but now the time had come to assail the lair of ironclad generals. Whereas I had waltzed into and out of the other temples with no sign of spiritual opposition, I knew the epicenter would be different.

—————

"Has anybody ever prayer-walked the temple in the center of the city?"

The Indian missionary frowned. His charge included a mixed group of Americans, Europeans and believers from south and northeast India, and he had invested the past thirty years of his life in this soil. "We do prayer-walking," he admitted, "but we don't go into the temples, and certainly not that one! To my knowledge no believer has ever been inside. It wouldn't be wise."

"Well," I declared, "the Lord has told me to go in there. We don't have to sing or worship out loud. Our presence as representatives of the One who came to free the captives is sufficient. Will your group join me?"

He shook his head. "The Lord hasn't told us to go inside temples. No one should do that unless the Lord clearly guides them, and apparently He's guiding you. So I wish you well. Let us know what happens!"

We parted on friendly terms, but the third excursion into the bowels of darkness would again be effectuated in the lone company of my Beloved.

On the day of my attempt to enter the epicenter, I didn't bring my cycle, because cycles parked in that part of town might not be there when you returned, matter not how strong a chain or cable they be locked with. Though in appearance scrawny, the little man pedaling my rickshaw wheeled his charge expertly through the streets at a fairly good clip, aiming the wheels to miss the largest potholes. His shoulder protruded through a threadbare shirt, and with each downward step on the right pedal, a tear in the worn-out seat of his pants exposed a glimpse of underwear.

Buried deep in the contiguous maze of ancient buildings, the epicenter was accessible by several alleys too narrow for a four-wheeled vehicle or even a tri-wheeled rickshaw. I disembarked the rickshaw at the triune-spired archway marking the entrance to the main approach. Worshipers intent on reaching the temple and shopkeepers peddling pagan paraphernalia jammed the long, narrow passageway. Above, gangs of screeching, fighting, defecating monkeys galloped across rickety tin awnings and swung from tangled masses of illegal electric wires.

The nearer I approached, the more pungent the spiritual atmosphere grew. Blank-faced supplicants chanted or muttered praises to the gods while they walked, and cassette players droned out mantras crafted to numb the mind and draw it toward nothingness. The temple entrance, spanning a width of four feet, was guarded by tan-suited policemen toting WWII-era Lee-Enfield rifles. Their eyes followed each corpus that stepped across the threshold.

While yet far enough removed to avoid attracting the attention of the guards, I flattened myself against one side of the lane. Stuck to the wall like a camouflaged moth, I could assess my approach without being trampled by the relentless flow of humanity.

Directly opposite the entrance gaped a pitch-black cavern housing an idol to which devotees offered clay bowls bearing a squat flaming candle. Those entering past the guards bore in their hands an offering to be laid before the idols. I wondered if my lack of offering would be questioned.

Strewn up and down the lane on either side of the entrance lay sandals and shoes, removed by the devotees in respect for the idols. I would remove mine as a declaration that "wherever the soles of my foot shall tread" the people in bondage would be set free.

A ledge protruding from a wall provided a bit of a hiding place under which I stuffed my sandals, hoping they would still be present upon my return. Beneath my bare feet the stone pavement oozed with a slimy concoction of Ganges water and mud. Slipping and sliding my way along the corridor to join the end of the line, I noticed something that indicated my task might be more difficult than expected. Over the entrance hung a sign. Half-concealed by dusty spiderwebs and fly dung but nonetheless undeniably legible, it read ENTRY OF NON-HINDUS STRICTLY PROHIBITED.

Already standing in the line along with the others shuffling toward the entrance, the guard had seen me by now. The shopkeepers and police can spot a foreigner no matter how well-disguised. I resolved to attempt the feat of blending in, and if questioned, to play dumb and act as if I hadn't seen the sign.

"She looks almost Indian," Vincent had crowed on several occasions when questioned how his family dared harbor a foreigner in their home. Admittedly my Italian tan, petite stature, near-black hair and *salwar* dress carried me far toward acceptance as one of the natives. That which had won the hearts of the Indian believers, though, was how I had lived among them, eating their food, drinking their water and enduring their sufferings. "No foreigner ever loved us this way," they had said. "So," they continued, "you aren't a foreigner, you're one of us."

Years later my Hindi would attain such *deshi* fluidity as to confuse the cashiers at tourist attractions. I made a game of gaining admittance for the Indian price of Rs. 20 instead of the foreigner price of Rs. 350. Indian friends applauded whenever I declared, using the colloquial words and intonations that can only be acquired by living with the natives, "My face may be that of a foreigner but my heart is Indian!"

But at this moment, to open my mouth would instantly identify me as an outsider on a covert mission with no intention of worshiping the idols.

My ticket past those guards would have to be issued by miraculous intervention.

The line inched along, and I kept my head down and my eyes straight ahead. My turn to cross the threshold into the temple arrived. Upon lifting my foot to take the final step that would put me inside, a guard barred my path with his rifle. *"Rukho!"* he shouted, glowering at me from under his hat. "Tourist no entry. Look at sign!" He pointed at the cobwebby plaque above. "Go! Go from here!"

Thus thwarted was my first attempt to enter the epicenter.

The second attempt, initiated a week later, met the same rebuff with a leveled Lee-Enfield.

"God," I opined, "You told me to go in there, so this is Your problem, not mine. You have to get me inside."

Many weeks passed before I felt it was time to make a third attempt. Setting out in the wee hours of the morning, I soon found myself amidst a dense throng of humanity pressing their bodies toward the epicenter. I soon learned this happened to be the day when the entire city turned out to do obeisance to the deity called Destroyer.

Bodies packed as tight as upright sardines jammed the lane from wall to wall. After over an hour of jostling and pushing and being carried along with the flow like a stick in whitewater, I again approached that ominous doorway. There stood the guards with their Lee-Enfields. But this time it wasn't an orderly line that the police could easily control. The mob seethed forward, pushing and shoving in desperation to gain proximity to the idols on this auspicious day, and the police were challenged to avoid being bowled over. In the moment that I reached the entrance, two ladies directly ahead of me thrust themselves inside. Simultaneously I put my head down like a bull, drove my shoulder in between them and hurled myself over the threshold. In India, personal space is nonexistent, especially in crowds, wherefore the ladies paid me no heed.

I found myself triumphantly inside, having escaped the eyes of the guards.

There at last I stood, in the citadel of the warlords, having penetrated the epicenter, the hub from which the chains of bondage radiated across the land. Authorized by the rightful King, I must now execute the acts that would release the power of that King to liberate the captives held in bondage for millennia.

For a moment I stood there, taking in the atmosphere. It was as if I had passed from Planet Earth into another dimension, another realm.

Arrayed around the circular area were images of varying size and shape. Some were dingy gray or black with grotesque faces and wild eyes. Phallic symbols were peppered throughout, large and small, unashamedly displaying an upright penis copulating with a vagina. Most, however, conveyed the outward appearance of cheer or peace. Their faces displayed an alluring softness of utmost bliss, eyes half-closed, a hand lifted in benediction. Decked with jewelry and ornaments, the images portrayed happiness and material blessing. Devotees bowed before the idols, offering incense, coconuts and bananas, pouring milk and *ganga jal* upon the phalluses and garlanding them with marigolds.

Yet the people's faces ranged from blank hopelessness to desperation. They cried out to the stone idols, pleading for them to hear and have mercy, bright *saris* of the women contrasting with their ashen countenances.

The oblations of previous worshipers putrefied in the sweltering heat, and the overflow of milk and water along

with banana peels and coconut husks and discarded marigolds transformed the floor into a morass of filth. The lifeless idols with wide, staring eyes could neither consume the
offerings nor answer the people's prayers, and centuries of
tradition along with the spirits invoked by the leaders held
them in bondage. The chains I had beheld in the dream
bound them. They were being dragged down, down into
death and oblivion. Each one, the priests included, was
enslaved.

Then I knew that, despite the milling masses of humanity
ringing bells and conducting rituals and priests leading them
in mantras, none were truly alive. They were living a form of
death, entwined in the warlords' chains. The most truly alive
creatures in this place were the hordes of flies that swirled
about and congregated on the idols and the floor, gorging
themselves on the mess. A cruel mockery, the people whom
God created and loved had come here hoping to receive salvation and freedom, but instead they received bondage while
insects feasted upon their desperation.

Slicing through the drone of chanting voices and buzzing
flies, a piercing voice called out—a summons. The people inside the temple stampeded to the center and clustered around
a silver barricade. The high priest had arrived to conduct the
ceremony for which the people had come. Positioned directly
beneath the golden dome and protected by the ornate barricade was a black stone phallus so heavily swathed with
wreaths of marigolds as to be virtually obscured. Over it
hung a copper pot releasing a steady drip of milk.

As the priest began to chant, the people mimicked while
he sprinkled them with Ganges water. The people strained
forward, believing that if the water touched their flesh their
sins would be cleansed and they would be spared an eternity

of torment or escape being reincarnated as a dog or a Dalit outcaste.

I gave My blood for them, I heard my Beloved affirm. *My resurrection defeated the darkness, but still the enemy's hood is sealing their ears and eyes. The time has come for them to hear and see. You are a carrier of My authority. Proclaim liberty to the captives!*

Then I noticed, through the spiritual thickness of the atmosphere, something else lived in the room. A presence more alive than the dead images, more alive than the priest or the people and more alive than the flies. High up in the smoke-blackened cupola and peering out from behind each idol, beings lurked. Creatures sinister and ancient and dark— the principalities that had reigned here unchallenged for the past three millennia. The warlords I had seen in the dream. Unseen yet more real than flesh, their eyes stared at me from the spiritual realm with shock, fear and rage. Shock that an ambassador of their enemy had penetrated their long-sequestered command center. Fear because I represented the true King, who had defeated them long ago, and rage that a human would dare challenge them.

I had awakened the warlords from the deep. They were now aware of my presence, and I of theirs.

It was time to do business.

Energy and fire rose up in me, as I stepped in front of one of the idols and began to speak, quietly but nonetheless audibly, the praises of the true King and the victory of His atoning death and resurrection. Asserting the authority vested in me as His ambassador and officer, I proclaimed the liberty of these captives here in this temple, this city, this nation and beyond. I moved to one idol after another, then stretched out the same proclamation over the cauldron of activity directly under the golden dome. Upon the territory where countless millions of chained slaves of darkness had stood and bowed to their slave drivers, I placed my feet as a testimony of the presence and victory of the Liberator of slaves and the Author of life. Positioned and authorized to be an emancipator and abolitionist, I declared, "In Jesus' name, let God's people go!"

In the Spirit, I sensed great roots of darkness being cut as if with a massive ax. Chains were breaking and a heavy canopy lifting, and light was filtering in. The power of darkness over the land had been weakened. The possibility now existed for the people to soon be able to hear and receive the liberating love of Jesus and its accompanying freedom from poverty, sickness and slavery.

After thoroughly addressing the principalities residing beneath the dome, I knew my job was done and my purpose for coming here had been fulfilled. With a sense of transcendence, I exited, reclaimed my sandals and returned home.

But the warlords would not tolerate the invasion of their lair without retaliating.

That night began no differently than other nights had as I lay down on the thin mat on the floor that constituted my bed. The incessant honking of horns out on the street, which I'd long since come to ignore, was drowned out by the pounding drums of a wedding procession making its halting, traffic-jamming way down a street to the wedding lawn. There, Bollywood dance hits would boom through massive speakers till after midnight. But even this couldn't postpone my slumber. Today had been a great day of victory. So with complete peace, I drifted off to sleep.

"WE'RE GOING TO DESTROY YOU!"

My eyes flew open and I sat bolt upright.

Jaws gaping, yellow fangs gleaming with drool, a mob of horrific demon faces swooped toward me. So near were their leathery hides I could see the folds and creases and their bodies plated with armor. Their breath spewed burning sulfur, and their great hairy claws reached out, hungry, loathing, ghastly, going straight for my throat.

There was no time to think. My arm shot out, finger leveled at the advancing horde. I shouted, "STOP IN JESUS' NAME!"

They fell backward as if pummeled by a massive invisible fist. Confused and enraged, they milled about, squabbling amongst themselves. Then they regrouped and attacked again. With the same command I opposed them and they were repulsed. After a few more tries the demons left.

Thrilled and awed both at how effectively my intrusion into the temple had riled up the spiritual realm, and at how deftly the name of Jesus repelled them, I praised my Beloved for giving us such power over the forces of darkness, and returned to my slumber.

"YOU CAME INTO OUR TERRITORY! NOW WE'RE GOING TO DESTROY YOU!"

They were coming at me again! Again I rebuked them. This happened three or four times throughout the night, but not once were they able to touch me. Each time I rebuked them they were forced to stop and back off. It was an intense but thrilling encounter.

This level of spiritual warfare, however, is taxing on the human body. Upon waking in the morning, I was extremely ill. For one week the most severe combination of fever, aches and nausea beset me—a backlash of the battle with the warlords.

Spiritual darkness is real, and spiritual warfare is real. I had delved to the root of the chains binding the people in slavery, and there planted, as it were, a stick of dynamite to blast open the prison doors of the demonic underworld. The discharge had torn apart some of the fortress moorings. Some of the warlords' chains had snapped. Turmoil had invaded the realms of darkness.

What was next?

Surely I would now begin to function as a proper emissary. Instead of traipsing around helping others, at last I would be released into the real action. In the steps of those having gone before me, I supposed I would learn the Hindi language and begin to build friendships with the people who didn't yet know Christ—the pastoral villagers tilling the fields and the devout who frequented the Ganges and the peddlers along the road. I would talk with them of my Beloved, lead them into a relationship with Him and start fellowship groups in which I would teach them the Bible. This was what my superiors had taught me. This was the model followed by the missionary societies. I therefore supposed that in the wake of this preparatory season of spiritual chain-breaking, I would soon be following their lead. I would soon be the one to rescue the people out of darkness.

But my Beloved had radically different plans.

One day while I walked down a street, He spoke with re-sounding clarity. His statement provoked in me two equally unhappy feelings—shock and disappointment.

You shall not act or intervene in the traditional way, He charged me. *You will not travel much into the villages. Your face won't often be seen preaching and teaching. Instead, you will serve the native believers. They are My chosen vessels who will bring light to the villages. They will be emissaries to their own people.*

For weeks I besieged God with complaints.

"What did You send me all the way over here for anyway, to sit in an office?"

"So what is my job then, to waste away in the background and let others have all the fun?"

"You mean I'll hardly ever pray for the sick and see them recover? You mean I won't be out there among the crowds, leading people to a relationship with You? You mean I won't be the one to teach new believers Your Word?"

He declined to answer.

Ever since the dramatic Encounter, in which I had seen Him in the hour of His suffering, the highest honor and greatest high I could imagine would be the indescribable privilege of enduring persecution for the name of Jesus. But "serving the native believers" involved primarily support roles and behind-the-scenes activities, which meant I would be generally exempt from persecution. So I complained, "You mean I won't be chased out of villages and stoned and beat up and put in jail? I won't join You in suffering for people's freedom?"

In response to these arguments, He was gentle and patient. I continued to go out into the villages with Vincent, Munulal, JD and Krishna. I observed their effectiveness when they brought the Gospel to new villages and saw the miraculous healing of diseases. One day news arrived that Saroj and his family had been accepted back into their village. We rejoiced together to learn that some who saw the video had persevered in their commitment to Jesus. Saroj had since then led several of his neighbors to faith, and the house from which they had been evicted now served as the venue for a weekly home fellowship and Bible study.

When the local believers told their simple story of languishing in the fear of demons and slavery to witch doctors and then how they discovered liberty and joy and peace through Jesus, it made a far greater impact than my own dramatic account of seeing Jesus face-to-face. My story, matter not how sensational, was still the experience of a foreigner, a transplant from another dimension. But JD's, Munulal's, Isha's, Krishna's and Saroj's stories were the experiences of their fellow Indian villagers, familiar brothers and sisters. Able to relate personally to their own, the people's hearts opened wide and they realized that they could also have the liberty and freedom enjoyed by their own native kinsmen.

Language and song proved potent as well. Messages delivered in the village dialect were readily received, while the same message spoken in the trade language of Hindi garnered a lukewarm response. When I led Hindi choruses on my guitar, the people patiently sang along, the words falling out of their mouths limp and lacking gusto. But then JD and Munulal struck up one of JD's recently composed village *bhajans*. This original musical style had been cherished by the villagers for centuries. By it the Hindu legends passed from generation to generation in a largely oral culture, and unschooled agrarian people entertained themselves with neither television nor city lights. Now the form was being redeemed, the same musical style filled with rich accounts of the living God of love and compassion. A man who wasn't yet a believer enthusiastically banged on a *dholok* drum, and another jangled a rhythm on a tambourine, and another pumped a harmonium while JD belted out the semi-melodious verses. At the sound of their own heart music, the audience sprang alive. Great beaming smiles spread across the drawn leathery faces. Exuberant shouts enlivened the air, and hands shot up, and the atmosphere bubbled with joy and celebration.

The light dawned. Now flashing in my psyche with a glint of buoyant anticipation beamed the revelation: "Natives are the key! I must be a servant of the native believers. I am to help them grow into humble, confident, anointed ambassadors of the King. I am to stand behind them with provision and strategy. They will take His message to the villages. I will empower them to do so. Together we will be a dynamic team, each fulfilling that for which he or she was best equipped. The native believers comprise the strategy to a whole new dimension of rescuing captives."

But who would lead the charge? Possessing little education, the new believers were barely capable of reading. Sharing the elementary Gospel message with their fellow villagers and leading a small house-based church pushed their capacity to its limits. My assignment to enlighten and liberate the masses of north India would require a person of some reasonable education. The person must be a native of north India. He must be a true general, not afraid of the warlords and committed to penetrate dark places to set captives free. He must also walk in divine anointing, a person whom God had, like me, prepared and called to this specific mission.

The odds against my finding such a leader consigned the task to the realm of the miraculous.

The necessity to start an organization had also been knocking around in my head. If I was to assist the natives, that meant I must bring new believers into training programs and send them out to villages. I must equip them with cycles, Bibles and ministry tools. For this to be possible, others must catch the vision. If the Lord's plan wasn't limited to just little ol' me out here doing my personal best, if a team was to be developed, then the next step involved registering a nonprofit.

Soon afterward, with Mom's help doing all the bookwork on the U.S. side, TellAsia Ministries was formed. Our mission would bring hope, salvation and liberation both spiritually and physically to India and beyond—and do so by mobilizing the few existing native believers as ambassadors to their own people.

Mystery now fluttered like an excited bird. A portal had opened and a shaft of light shone through, illuminating a secret corridor. I was nigh on to entering a revolutionary new dimension—a dimension in which my Beloved and I, together with the native people, would rescue the ragged treasures.

5

Treasure Hunting

"The kingdom of heaven is like treasure hidden in a field. When a man found it, he hid it again, and then in his joy went and sold all he had and bought that field."

Matthew 13:44

*P*CO, STD, ISD" painted in red and green over a background of bright orange consumed the entire side of the phone booth. A red rotary phone and calculator occupied the counter inside. Behind the counter a wizened operator worked his mouth, red seepage escaping his cracked lips betraying the fact he had gone a bit overboard on his helping of *paan*. A customer, finishing his phone call, handed the receiver back to the operator and counted out four coins. His young son, eyes fixated on a jar of candy in the nearby general store, pulled at his father's pant leg and begged for a rupee.

These routine proceedings screeched to a halt the moment I entered. Plunking my backpack on the only chair, I extracted my paraphernalia—an IBM laptop weighing in at eight pounds, a card modem and a black rubber listener contraption resembling a telephone handset with cord. The little boy forgot about the candy, and the men stopped their transaction to stare wide-eyed at what to them equated futuristic technology out of a science-fiction film, or a bomb.

I cast them a reassuring smile and opened the laptop lid. When the screen lit up, they sighed with relief, and fearful stares relaxed into fascinated chattering. I set the laptop on the table by the phone. Not bothering to attempt to explain, I inserted the modem, clamped the listener device onto the red phone handset with a wide piece of Velcro and plugged it into the modem.

Desiring to speak to me, the operator leaned over to the rusty bars on the window of his shop and spat. A red stream spattered against the opposite wall. "What are you doing?" he queried in Hindi.

"Internet. Email," I replied. "Don't worry, it will register on your machine as a local call."

A good deal of skill was required to put a phone call through the primitive and overloaded lines, and operators prided themselves in timing switch hook and dial just right to connect calls. But connecting to the internet had to be done entirely from the computer.

One hand on the track point mouse, the other on the phone switch hook, I opened the dial-up dialog on the computer, pressed and released the switch hook, then clicked Dial.

The dial tone was marred by static.

The operator fiddled with the cord.

Static.

He disconnected my listening device and beat the receiver on the table, extracting a good bit of dust. I reconnected the listening device.

More static.

From beneath the table he procured a second phone, and I connected the black listener to it.

At last a clear dial tone. I sighed with relief when variegated beeps indicated the modem was dialing. Then the ring . . . and then a busy signal.

Try again.

Busy.

I fiddled with the listening device. If it wasn't clamped tightly up against the handset, outside noise would mess up the connection.

Fourth try.

Busy.

Fifth.

At long last the welcome sight of blinking computers in my lower right screen indicated I had penetrated all opposing elements and reached cyberspace. I rushed to the email program and clicked Send/Receive. It took over two minutes for one 4 KB email to come in. Two emails—three—then the connection died.

Dial again.

Success.

One more email and one sent.

Connection died.

Dial again.

After an hour I had succeeded in downloading five emails and had sent three.

One was from Mom.

"Dad's prostate cancer spread into his bones. He has a morphine patch to reduce the pain. Come home soon."

After engineering the grand arena in Minnesota, Dad and Mom had built two final homes for a total of eight in 31 years. Perched on a hill looking out across the blue-green slopes of Appalachia, this homestead was twelve miles from the bigger-than-small-town of Cleveland, Tennessee—as nigh to civilization as the Cinquantas had ever situated themselves, yet still comfortably remote.

With the sale of the arena, Alpenglow assumed an honorific post as cherished dressage schoolmaster for a longtime friend whose Christian riding stable provided both fun and spiritual guidance to young people. But when my folks moved to this new location, Alpindia, Alpen's third foal, untrained, had lived in the pasture below the hill.

After my initial season along the Ganges, I had set out across India and come upon a pastor who had been praying for a Jeep. He had identified a used vehicle equipped with neither power steering nor AC, and the driver's seat was welded in place so that the driver's knees bumped the bottom of the steering wheel. But to this man of God, the Jeep might as well have been a Lexus. To own it comprised an impossible dream that, if brought to reality, would enable deeper penetration of light into dark territory.

The prohibitive expense of international calling relegated such to the rare splurge or emergency, but I dialed the double zeroes and announced to Mom, "Sell Alpindia, we're buying a Jeep." The filly sold for $4,000—exactly the cost of the vehicle. Because of the Jeep, hundreds of Maharshtran men driving carts pulled by great white oxen with orange-painted horns, and ladies with extra-long *saris* tied up between their legs scrubbing steel pots with mud, received the hope and freedom of the Gospel.

The sale of Alpindia represented the surrender of my last earthly possession. I had given everything for the vision and for the call of my Beloved. Back home for the summer, I stood gazing out from the porch at the empty, overgrown pasture and knew that I had done all I could do alone. From here on, others must believe in this vision and help rescue the captives chained in darkness.

Having registered TellAsia Ministries a few months earlier, Mom had plunged into a new career as voluntary one-woman CEO, development director, scheduler and bookkeeper. At age 58 she took classes and learned how to use the computer, including how to make newsletters on Microsoft Publisher and track finances in Excel. One side of our living room was transformed into an office with a long desk, computer, cubbyholes and shelves for paperwork and a spacious filing cabinet. Bimonthly Mom formatted the stories and the pixilated early digital photos I sent from India into an elaborate newsletter. Then she printed it on the extra-wide bubble jet made to handle tabloid-size documents, folded, addressed, stuffed, sealed, sorted by zip code for bulk mail and carted the finished envelopes to the PO. She phoned our old friends, twice-removed relatives and anybody to whom we had ever tipped our hat. She informed them of her daughter's ministry and asked if they wanted to receive the newsletter. She compiled copious pages of handwritten lists of people and contacts and wrote thank-you notes to everyone who gave even five dollars.

Her tireless efforts paid off, and soon the $200-a-month income on which I had been managing began to grow.

She had scheduled a ministry tour that would route me from Tennessee up to old friends in Wisconsin and Minnesota, out to meet other family and friends in Kansas and Colorado, then around to Texas and down to Georgia and Florida and at last back to Tennessee. Having paid $700 for a 1970 Tercel whose odometer read 208,000 miles, I set out on my first speaking tour, staying with friends and pastors' families, finding my way to tiny backwoods churches with a map open on the steering wheel and presenting the work in India on a manual carousel-slide projector. In those days 75 cents bought a gallon of gas. By the end of six months, I had traveled twenty thousand miles. Besides gas, I spent not a single penny excepting one splurge on Micky D's. I raised the grand sum of $6,000—meager, but a start.

Dad's health was rapidly deteriorating. Along with running the fledgling TellAsia office, Mom nursed him and grieved as his life waned. When his hospice bed was raised a bit, he could turn to the left and look out at the beautiful mountain vista. Or he could turn to the right and watch Mom at work across the room on the computers. A special lift over the bed enabled Mom to raise him up and swing him over onto a Porta-Potty. Hospice visited daily to bathe him and give him an enema. His hours passed in a stuporous, drugged sleep, induced by the morphine that kept the claws of pain at bay.

Dinnertimes were strange now. Dad's dope-encased fingers would no longer fiddle with the TV dials to view *Hogan's Heroes*. There would be no more fighting the Nazis and laughing at Colonel Klink and Sergeant Schultz. We ate our dinner in mournful gloom. Mom and I even missed his usual gruff complaints that the food was cold or overcooked or not salted enough. A sense of sadness pervaded the house, the certainty of death drawing near bereft from the confidence of life beyond the grave.

Dad had heard the message of Jesus multiple times, and ever since my departure to India had read his Bible and attended church with Mom. Even so, Dad had yet to indicate he had confessed Jesus as his Lord. When a pastor visited, to his Gospel presentation Dad growled his typical response, "I've been a good guy, never hurt nobody. God won't send me to hell. Now, change the subject, will ya?"

Autumn was nearing, along with the time when I would have returned to India. Upon indicating my intention to postpone my trip so as to be with him in his final hours, Dad had stated firmly, "I don't want you to stay and watch me die." He insisted that I go back to India and proceed to grow the ministry.

I knew I wouldn't see him alive again in this life. Would I see him in heaven? I felt compelled to know where he was spiritually. Would the man who had nurtured me and instilled in me a priceless foundation of overcoming confidence, who had given everything for me and for others, at last fail to receive the greatest treasure of all—an eternity of peace and joy in heaven with God?

On a lazy afternoon two days before my departure for India, my answer would come. Mom was napping in the bedroom, and Dad, semi-awake with his bed raised a bit and several pillows under his head, gazed tiredly out the window. I sat down beside him and took his hand, once strong and calloused and covered with airplane dope, now soft and cold and limp.

"Dad," I began, "I love you and there's something I must know. You asked me to go back to India and not stay for you. That's fine. But you must tell me something first."

189

His eyelids opened wider, the pupils glassy but alert, and his hand squeezed mine ever so faintly.

The time was upon me. I dreaded the usual response, the gruff rebuttal that would reveal he had not yet accepted the Gospel message. But I had to know. To know, I must ask the most critical question in the universe.

"Dad, please tell me—when you die, *why* do you believe you'll be in heaven?"

Time went into suspend. A tangible weightiness enveloped the room and a silence broken only by the ticking of the wall clock. His glassy eyes shifted askance, and his hand loosened its clasp on mine. He turned his head toward the other side of the room, the office area. Then slowly, painfully he rolled to where he could see the computer.

On the computer, idle at the time, a screen saver played over and over—a silhouette of Jesus carrying the cross, then being thrown down on it, His hands nailed and the cross lifted vertical.

Dad raised a shaky finger and pointed. "I'll be in heaven . . . because of what He did."

I probably hadn't breathed for over a minute, but at this response, I drew a deep sigh of relief combined with awe. Dad was saved. He had accepted the fact that his good works could not save him, but only the righteousness and redemption received by faith in our substitute and advocate, Jesus. Dad would be in heaven. God's grace and love had triumphed. The stifling suspense lifted, along with the sense of dread and death in the room. His soon-approaching physical departure would not be an end or a tragedy to grieve, but a release from pain and suffering and an entrance into eternal life and endless joy. One day we would meet again, in the glory and radiance of eternal life.

Not long afterward, Joe Cinquanta passed away at age 81—aeronautical genius, architectural craftsman, mechanical wizard, personification of freedom, authentic American pioneer born one hundred years late and the father who infused into me the nonexistence of "impossible."

King David

The dark corridors of the dilapidated building would have resembled catacombs had they been underground. Windowless walls with peeling paint contained room after tiny room made of raw bricks stuck together with eroding mortar. The sullied glow of a few bulbs dangling from up above revealed cords thickened by a conglomerate of fly excrement, cobwebs and dust.

From the squalid floor strewn with garbage, dirt, red *paan* spittle, goat droppings and discarded bits of yarn, a naked balloon-bellied toddler retrieved her fallen biscuit. Black bits of filth and a few hairs adhered to the half-eaten edge. With hands that had been everywhere all day without a washing, she shoved the works into her mouth.

The mother, barely nineteen, paid her no heed. Straining her eyes through the dingy yellow light, she continued passing colorful threads in and out between vertical strings held taut by beams at top and bottom. On either side of her worked the rest of her family. Her husband's forehead glistened with sweat, eyes empty and blank. Her two older children stopped long enough to look around, caught sight of me and became transfixed at the wonder of a visitor from the outside world. Their bashful eyes asked, *Are you here to help us?*

191

Thread by thread a lovely ornate blue and gold rug emerged from the lower beam. Its value trumping what one of these families earned from an entire year of toil, the rug would soon grace the marble floor of a sheik's palace or the master bath of an American aristocrat. Its beauty and its destination mocked the misery of its makers.

Then I was drawn into their world—a world in which, when your baby cries, you have nothing to give her but water, or tea with a dribble of milk. A world where shopping means a visit to the dumpster. A world with no welfare, food stamps, sick days, Social Security, Medicare or Medicaid. Where a piece of fruit is a rare luxury and meat is out of the question. Where sickness lurks around every corner. A few days out of work could put this whole family on the street, turned out from their shelter and sole hope of making a livelihood. Unable to earn enough to ever own land, they would slave away in this cave until they sank into the squalor, wasted and used up.

"We come here from Nepal since one year. This is our home now." Gopal, a new believer and student in TellAsia's first discipleship class, had begged me to come see where he and his wife lived and worked on the outskirts of town.

He lingered behind a row of bent backs laboring on another loom. "This is Pramila, my wife." Gopal smiled with pride as one of the women acknowledged us. Apart from the sweat wetting her neck and the grime hastily wiped from her face with the tattered end of her *sari*, Pramila exemplified Asian beauty.

A searing pang of grief struck me. One word separated this woman from Miss Nepal—opportunity. Miss Nepal surely had no greater beauty, but she possessed what this young woman didn't: wealth and a good education. What separated the ragged malnourished rug factory child from a chubby, powdered, diapered baby in the developed world? Was one worth less and the other worth more? Was one good and the other bad, one important and the other unimportant? No. There was only one difference. Opportunity. One had opportunity to be well fed and well cared for and to go to a top-notch school and to earn a good living and to live in comfort. The other had no opportunity and was thus doomed to misery.

Gopal and Pramila led me down the hall past loom after loom and up a steep, narrow stairwell. Then along another corridor to a skuzzy curtain, the only partition between the public area and a tiny room—their room, it turned out. I paused long enough to lose the sandals, a practical etiquette preventing at least a few molecules of squalor from being tracked into the living area.

The room provided meager privacy. The goings-on of the family across the hall were clearly visible beneath the curtain while the hallway ruckus of children running and screaming, people shouting and beyond the walls, dogs barking and fighting and the unending honking of horns eliminated any scant sense of homeliness.

Furnishings were bare-bones. The bed consisted of a mat on the floor with its original red color faintly showing through ground-in layers of grime, inexorable despite vigorous scrubbing. No wider than a zipped sleeping bag, I could hardly imagine how two people might fit on it. Neatly stacked on the floor in a corner lay a few pots and pans along with the usual mud hearth.

Chattering excitedly to Gopal in unintelligible Nepali while casting shy glances at me, Pramila squatted before the hearth and fanned a tiny flame beneath twigs and patties of dried cow dung. Pouring water into a pan from a scavenged bottle and a dribble of milk from a plastic bag, the essential chai was under way. Gopal bustled around trying to find an additional cushion, hoping to make his guest as comfortable as possible on the red-black mat.

"Why did you leave Nepal?" I asked in Hindi. "Surely life couldn't have been worse there."

"Nepal no work," replied Gopal. "Here we earn a little money. Also Indian rupee worth more than Nepali rupee. But best news . . ." He reached for a plastic bag so worn that the printing had faded, carefully folded around its contents. He lifted it gently as if it contained a fragile flower or a priceless vase, and withdrew a Bible. "We find Jesus!" He hugged the black plastic-covered book to his breast. "Here we find peace. No peace before. In Nepal village we have so much fear. Everywhere bad spirits. They trouble us and make us sick and our gods no help us."

Seeing an opportunity to test how well he'd listened to my lesson in the discipleship class, I asked, "Do followers of Jesus have to fear the bad spirits anymore?"

"No!" He beamed. "No more fear. Jesus give us power. Now I tell spirits go away and they go!" He waved his arm as if throwing a rat against the wall.

"Why do they go? Where does the power come from?" I probed.

"From Jesus. From Him resurrection! Jesus win victory, now at Jesus' name every knee bow down and every tongue tell He is Lord!"

"Good! Full marks!" I applauded. "That's only the beginning. Now, what is your vision?" I queried. "What is God leading you to do when you finish the Bible class in a few weeks?"

"My people need Jesus. They are sad because of poor. But I'm not poor anymore because I have Jesus. Jesus love my people and He use me to help them."

"How will you help them?"

"I can teach them Bible, but where?" He cast a doleful glance across the room. "So small."

"How many people can sit here?" I asked. "Count. Tell me."

With a slightly distressed look, he began counting imaginary people seated on the floor. "Twenty people," he concluded.

"So?" I laughed. "There's a house church! Great. When you have this room full, then you can move it out into the hallway."

Gopal brightened. "Okay. We will have church meeting, and I teach Bible so they also follow Jesus!"

I turned to Pramila. "Sister, can you read and write?"

Shyly covering her mouth with her *sari*, the chocolate-skinned Barbie glanced questioningly at her husband.

"Go ahead, talk to her!" Gopal encouraged.

"Yes."

"Do you know only Nepali, or Hindi too?"

"Nepali . . . and some Hindi."

"How many of these children here attend school?"

"Maybe half," replied Gopal. "Some have to work along with parents, others play and do mischief."

"So while your husband teaches Bible study," I enjoined Pramila, "you can teach their children to read."

Her eyes sparkled and she dared to lower the *sari* from her mouth. "Me, teach?"

"Why not? You know how to read, they don't, and nobody else is teaching them. You're an educated woman and you can make a difference!"

"Good idea!" Gopal beamed at his wife. "One time you told me you want to be a teacher, no?"

Pramila's smile conveyed more than words. The drudgery of her work now contained a bright spot. She might not have much, but the little she had would now give children the hope of a brighter future.

"We will help you," I assured them. "My team members will visit and help you, and soon this carpet factory will be full of joy and learning and hope."

Walking out through the corridors of the carpet factory that day, the light bulbs already shone more brightly and the walls looked less dingy and the floor less littered. The light of Jesus and of education could now penetrate another community in which there had been only darkness.

The problem of who would head up TellAsia's growing team of native leaders now commanded top priority. An Indian person, not a Westerner, would have to carry out the hands-on mentoring and oversight of these grassroots bearers of light, who now included not only Gopal and Pramila in the carpet factory, but also young believers in villages ranging from the eastern border of the state to the distant northwestern mountains near Tibet.

The coordinator of TellAsia's work in India could not already be engaged in ministry with another organization. That eliminated Vincent, who was fully employed by his agency from Mumbai.

The candidate must burn with passion to bring freedom and hope to the people of northern India. Some of my disciples qualified on that point. But a further requirement included a good education—college grad at least, and capable of speaking English. That eliminated my disciples and every native of the Ganges River area I'd met so far.

I decided to approach a man respected as the grandfather of the city's tiny Christian community. An Indian missionary who had come to these regions decades ago, Brother George would be able to guide me to a potential candidate. When I made known my intent to hire a manager for the fledgling organization, he brightened. "I'd love to help," he replied. "Please interview my son. Surely he's a superb candidate for this post."

A year ago George's eldest son, Anthony, had graduated from one of India's prestigious Bible colleges. He had been nurtured in a strong Christian upper-middle-class family in an urban environment, groomed in British etiquette through his father's visits to England and spoke impeccable textbook English. His vision was to follow in the footsteps of his father and be a teacher of the Bible.

Anthony and I took some ministry excursions together. We traveled to the villages and met with the young leaders, and I observed Anthony teaching and interacting with them. His eloquence in preaching followed hard on that of Spurgeon, and his maturity and leadership skills were immaculate. I thought, *This is incredible. God has given me the perfect coordinator for TellAsia's work in India.*

But the Lord's reply completely confounded and opposed everything I had observed. In the firm but gentle voice I had come to recognize and obey, He declared, *This isn't the one.*

When I asked why, He didn't offer to elaborate. No further explanation would be given. Only this one brief statement. But it was clear and unmistakable. By all appearances Anthony was aces, but God had not chosen him to be TellAsia's India coordinator.

Perplexed, I returned to Brother George. "Uhh . . . Anthony is a superior young man and a great preacher," I began. "I was truly impressed. But the Lord said he's not the one for this job. I'm sorry. . . . Can you recommend someone else?"

Brother George didn't have to consider long before replying, "Well, then, how about Naresh?"

Naresh was George's stepson. A graduate of the same Bible college and nurtured in the same quality Christian environment, he shared his brother's vision and passion for the ministry work.

I observed Naresh teaching a class in the discipleship program, and then we traveled together to a village church. He was smart, courteous, had a love for the people and could preach and lead exceptionally well.

But again the Lord said, *He's not the right one.*

Now I was downright embarrassed to return again to Brother George. God had not allowed me to select either of his sons and not a solitary reason had I to offer. How could I possibly face him and ask for further recommendations?

I contended with God on the matter. "Look, God," I argued. "Do You know where I'm at? This is not America. This is not England or South Korea or Kenya. This is northern India. Do you know how few Christians live here? Less than one percent! Did You hear me? Hardly a single Christian to choose from . . . and You're being *picky*?"

God did not reply.

The story of the prophet Samuel and the sons of Jesse floated across my mind. This was what Samuel likely experienced after seven of Jesse's eight sons were presented before him and Samuel had to tell their anxious papa, "The Lord has not chosen these" (1 Samuel 16:10).

But Samuel had the guts to ask Jesse if he had another son.

Steeling myself, I returned to Brother George. "I'm so sorry, but Naresh isn't the right one either," I muttered. "Are you sure there isn't another person you can recommend who has a little education and a vision for ministry?"

Now the graying pastor sat back in his chair and stroked his beard for a few moments. At last he sighed and spoke. "Well, there is one. He's a village boy and doesn't know English too well. He picked up a few words during Bible college."

"So he does know a little English, and has completed college?" I queried.

"Yes, six months ago he returned from the same institution Anthony and Naresh attended. He was the first native of this region to ever graduate."

This was sounding good, but I would not allow myself the luxury of excess optimism. God had rejected the first seven of the prophet Samuel's candidates and I was only on number three. . . .

"May I meet him?" I inquired. "Where does he live?"

"He's out in the village doing ministry," George replied. "I'll see if I can reach him by phone. Come tomorrow at two p.m. He can probably reach here by then."

The following day when I stepped past the curtain into Brother George's guest room, the young man seated on the sofa would not have in the natural commanded esteem.

Distinguishing a suburbanite from a villager is not difficult. The marks defining who is educated and who is not, who has the qualifications to sit behind a desk and who will forever toil behind a shovel, are readily evidenced. The rural dwellers typically appear scrawny and underfed from years of struggling to survive. Their clothes are worn, and their hands and feet calloused. In India these signs indicate lack of opportunity, lack of the educational foundation requisite of a management role.

Those fleshed-out from sufficient nutritious food, of smooth skin and sometimes lighter complexion and wearing spiffy clothes, possess the benefits of having been educated. Exhibiting the traits indicative of management potential, these qualify as viable hires for a post such as project leader or regional coordinator. Such were Anthony and Naresh.

However the young man before me did not fit the image of management, but of a rugged villager. Ripped as the rickshaw pullers from cycling miles to the villages, he clearly had not been shuffling papers in an office. His skin was chocolate, baked black from hours in the scalding sun. His feet in rubber flip-flops were dry and calloused. Though spotlessly clean, tattered threads around the collar of his thin shirt connoted prolonged financial straits that disallowed the sparing of even a few rupees.

But I hardly saw these traits. Instead my attention was captured and my senses suspended by his countenance. Spreading from ear to ear, revealing an endless row of gleaming white teeth, was the widest, most radiant and triumphant smile I had ever seen on a human face. It proclaimed confidence and victory. His eyes danced with a sense that, despite hardships, all things were possible. Despite his rugged features and unimposing, nigh emaciated physique, an immaterial glory surrounded him, filling the room with a sense of heaven.

Before my brain could shift into gear, before a word had transpired between myself and the young man beaming at me from the sofa, my Beloved spoke. With undeniable clarity, His voice boomed into my spiritual ears.

"THIS IS THE ONE."

By bestowing upon their son his given name, his parents had consecrated him to the chief deity—Destroyer. Though native to a nearby village, David (not his given name) hadn't grown up the typical village boy. Hailing from the respected Vaisha caste, his ancestors commanded greater wealth than any family in the region. Servants tilled their ample farmland assets, and they lived in the only house built with bricks and mortar instead of mud and thatch. So David had enjoyed a dignified middle-class childhood. His parents wished their son to carry forward the ancestral worship and fear of the traditional gods while also becoming, they hoped, a successful businessman. According to their surname, their divine destiny in life, ordained by the gods and perpetrated from generation to generation, was that of barbering. Thus his father, Bhodi Lal, generated additional income by operating a humble shaving and hairstyling shop. Though private school still posed an unscalable financial mountain for a middle-class rural family, David attended the local public school, where he learned only Hindi. Growing up in the middle of six siblings, his unusually privileged childhood included pocket money to buy kites and candy.

When David was fifteen, tragedy struck. His mother, Hirawati, fell ill, diagnosed with leprosy and liver failure. Bagful after bagful of various pills and potions crossed the threshold of the once-happy home, but her condition didn't improve. Bhodi Lal summoned the priest, who prayed and chanted to the gods and anointed her with water from the Ganges, but her condition continued to decline.

When the village witch doctor's potions and incantations only worsened her condition, Bhodi Lal made a radical decision: They would pick up and move far south to the Mumbai megapolis. There Hirawati could receive treatment in one of the most renowned hospitals in India, the children could attend a quality school and the family could start another barbershop to make ends meet.

But even the doctors in Mumbai failed to cure Hirawati. Day by day her health deteriorated. The doctors gave her a few weeks to live.

In their home village in north India, David's family had hardly ever heard the name of Jesus. They knew nothing except what floated to them through the surrounding culture—the paintings depicted Jesus as a blond-haired, blue-eyed Caucasian. The community assumed Jesus to be the god of the white people, because years ago white people had come and preached about Him. Therefore Jesus was "the foreigner's god" or "the white man's god" and not the least appealing to Indians, who had an ample supply of their own gods.

But Mumbai boasted a thriving Christian community, and one of these families learned of Hirawati's plight. "We will come to your home and pray for your wife and mother," they had offered.

Bhodi Lal reacted violently. "Traitors!" he roared. "Allies of the British, following the white man's religion. Let Hirawati die! We will have no business with a Christian!"

But David and his siblings didn't care about religion. They loved their mother and would do anything to save her life. Their gods had failed. The witch doctor had failed. Medicine had failed. Their mother was dying. They had nothing to lose. One night they carried Hirawati out of the house, put her in an auto rickshaw and took her to the Christian home. The family gathered around Hirawati, pallid, half-unconscious and barely breathing. They began to pray and call out to God in the name of Jesus. David and his siblings watched their mother with anxious hope. The Christians then began to sing and to worship the Lord.

After fifteen minutes Hirawati opened her eyes. David and his siblings cried out in amazement when she looked around and then sat up. That night Hirawati was completely and miraculously healed. Having witnessed the supreme power and love of Jesus, David and his sisters and younger brother followed Christ from that day onward.

But despite the dramatic healing of his wife, Bhodi Lal remained unwilling to tolerate the practice of Christian faith in his home. "You can either have Jesus or me, but not both. If you choose Jesus, then get out of my house!" he shouted. David's oldest brother chose to side with his father in opposing the new faith of David, his mother, two sisters and younger brother.

After a few weeks of tolerating verbal and physical beatings, Hirawati declared, "Fine. I'm going back to our village to tell our people of the living God who answers prayer!" Hirawati booked her train ticket and returned to the desolate north, where nary a soul had heard the name of Jesus.

Typical of the plight of rural women in those days, Hirawati hadn't attended school and could neither read nor write. Without the ability to study the Bible, how could she learn about Jesus and how could she teach others? Hirawati held a Bible in her hands and asked God to teach her how to read. Then she spelled out letters, then words, then sentences. She found the letters beginning to make sense. God was miraculously teaching her to read.

But she faced yet another challenge. In the Indian village it was culturally inappropriate for a married woman to travel to visit other villages and homes without her husband. Sitting alone in her house in a remote village with an audience of goats and geckos, with whom would she share the message of Jesus? God soon solved this problem as well. When the family had left five years before, the whole village knew that Hirawati was practically dead. They knew the disease ravaging her body had defeated the priests, the hospital and the witch doctor. This meant there was no hope for her.

Word travels rapidly in the villages. Hearing that Hirawati was not just alive but completely healed and had come back home, people supposed her to have attained goddess-hood. To her home they brought their diseased, their dying and their demon-possessed. Hopeless and helpless, having spent their last pennies on potions and *poojas*, they laid their distressed loved ones before Hirawati and watched to see what she would do. The people were shocked when, instead of chanting a pagan spell, Hirawati gently laid her hands on them and prayed in Jesus' name. Scores were healed. The villagers could be heard whispering the nickname "Jesus Shaman." Soon she was leading a Bible study group in her home. One after another her neighbors chose to follow Jesus and turned from idol worship.

Meanwhile, David was still in Mumbai. Changing schools is a costly and difficult affair in India, so he and his siblings had no choice but to stay on with their abusive father and older brother. Though his siblings took their faith underground, David eschewed compromise. His father hated him for his commitment to Christ. While David ate dinner, his father would come up from behind him and pour water on the food on his plate. Then he would smack him on the head and shout, "So you believe Jesus does miracles! Okay, let's see Him dry up the water! Let's see Him turn it into cream." These abuses were demoralizing, but David persevered in his faith.

One day David secretly attended a youth conference. There God spoke to him: *I'm calling you to do the ministry. You will not pursue a job in commerce, but return to north India and serve your people.*

That evening he felt obliged to inform his father, whose opposition of his faith had, until now, proved violent and demoralizing but—barely—tolerable. But when David's father heard that his son would not pursue business but rather social work and Gospel preaching, he was livid. "You worthless fool!" Bhodi Lal screamed. "You have brought shame on your family. You would have had a good future, but now you will ruin your life! You might as well go out and beg! I gave you everything to help you succeed. Now you intend to waste it!"

With these words Bhodi Lal unleashed his fury on David, beating him with fists and belt and whatever hard object he could snare. Hurling him bloodied and bruised out of the house and onto the street, Bhodi Lal locked the door.

From that time David dared go into the house only when his father was out. For days he survived on the street, a fugitive with nowhere to go. A Christian family took him in until he finished high school, whereupon he returned north to join his mother's ministry in the village.

Back in the north, David found his mother leading a burgeoning church. But her vision for her son extended beyond that of a village pastor. "Our entire region lies in darkness, superstition, fear and poverty," she said. "The people must be set free, and that work requires a strong and well-trained leader. I had no opportunity to be educated, so you must go to college and learn the Bible."

"But how can I go to college," David wondered, "since we have no money?"

With that Hirawati opened a box that she had kept secretly hidden throughout the years. Inside lay the gold jewelry from her wedding day. "Go." She pressed the weighty and finely crafted necklace, earrings and bracelets into his palm. "Sell this and go to college."

The great sacrifice of his mother's wedding jewelry sufficed to pay for David's first year in college. The lectures, books and exams were in English, and David knew hardly a word of English. He struggled and studied night and day. Slowly he began to learn English while also learning the Bible and other subjects.

When the money ran out, the college issued him a scholarship and he was allowed to continue his studies in exchange for work. At times he didn't even have paper on which to do his assignments and had to ask other students to give him a page from their notebooks. Sometimes he had no pencil and had to wait till other students had finished their assignments, then sit up throughout the night writing with a borrowed pencil.

After David's mother passed away and he had graduated from college, diverse and glowing offers passed his way.

"Stay here at the college and pursue your master's degree," one of the college leaders urged. "You represent our first graduate hailing from the darkest area of India. We will help pay for your studies. Soon you will have a job as a teacher."

"I'll pay your airfare to England," a visiting professor from London offered. "Come continue your studies in my seminary."

But to one after the other David had replied, "No, my calling is to my people here in north India and to the people in the villages. I must stay here and help bring them freedom and hope."

So David returned home to his village having gained an education, but having no source of income and no one to encourage or guide him. Then he received a call from his father. Bhodi Lal hadn't spoken to his son in years, so David was amazed to hear from him. Bhodi Lal informed David that he had arranged his marriage. Assuming that this meant his father had decided to accept and love him again as his son, David was ecstatic.

But after the marriage ceremony, he learned that he had been cruelly tricked. Bhodi Lal had maliciously chosen a sick girl to be David's wife with the intention of further tormenting him.

Growing up in a poor family, Renu had had no opportunity to go to school. Instead, a large portion of her childhood had been spent slaving over a smoky cow-dung fire inside a mud hut with no windows and no chimney. Day after day pollution had coursed through her young lungs, and she had succumbed to the dread disease of tuberculosis. Now she was dying.

At that point it would have been culturally acceptable for David to have refused to take her as his wife on the grounds of her undisclosed illness. Instead he chose to be faithful to the covenant. He took Renu home to the village and did his best to provide the costly medication she needed in hopes that she would pull through. Weekly he carried her on the bicycle twenty miles to and from the city to seek treatment at the public hospital. Despite his efforts, her health worsened.

Having persevered and trudged on despite one hardship and opposition after another, David cried out to God, "Lord, my life purpose is to bring Your freedom and grace to these villages. My people must discover the joy and peace and love that only Jesus can give. I must bring education to the children and put an end to the injustice and oppression. Please help me fulfill my calling."

It was at that time, while David faithfully did what he could to serve his people, though penniless, persecuted and enduring the tragedy of his wife's deteriorating condition, that Brother George summoned him to the city.

"There's an American lady here looking for a helper to lead a new organization," he informed. "You should come meet her."

That day marked the beginning of a great turnaround in David's life. After the Lord spoke to me saying, *This is the one*, I learned of Renu's medical situation, and TellAsia provided the necessary treatment for her to recover from TB. Soon afterward TellAsia shifted David from the village to a rented facility in the city, which would serve as our base of operations.

Through talking with David, I learned that he had been crushed and beaten down by the demoralizing circumstances and relentless onslaught of adversity. Thus he found it hard to believe he could walk in greater influence than a village pastor. But in that brokenness, humility and unshakable tenacity that was willing to die rather than yield to darkness, I knew were hidden the seeds of a mighty man of valor. "From now on I will call you David," I declared, "because God will raise you up to be a great leader, known and loved throughout this region. In authority and influence you will be King David for your people and will lead them to freedom and dignity."

The prophecy has been remarkably and beautifully fulfilled. Today, no-longer-scrawny "King" David is respected and loved throughout the region. He and the team of native leaders we developed together have introduced his people far and wide to the love and freedom found in the living God who heals and delivers and saves. With the backing of TellAsia, he has risked his life to deliver aid to tsunami victims, put himself in harm's way to protect and defend the persecuted and faced down pimps and mafia to rescue trafficked girls from the horror of brothels. Through his leadership we have launched education centers providing hope and a brighter future to thousands of village children and liberated unskilled youth from economic slavery by equipping them with vocational skills.

Thus under intense and crushing pressures, a treasure was formed, waiting in darkness for a chance to shine. The man who had been consecrated to serve the chief of the warlords would boldly raid their lair and lead thousands of slaves to life and liberty.

Addict to Ambassador

"Why can't you be a good man? We do sacrifices, priest do rituals, but no use. You still drink and steal and do every sort of foolishness. You bring shame to our family!" The words of his father, spoken out of love defeated by frustration from years of pointless effort, cut Alok's wounded heart deeper each time they cycled through his brain. Today the words refused to leave. They tormented him, thorns working their way deeper and deeper until they impaled his soul.

"Why can't you be a good man?"

Why can't I be a good man? The question taunted him, mocking his vain efforts to fulfill it. No matter with what degree of desperation he longed to be a good man, he couldn't. The cravings invariably won out; the power controlling him could not be resisted.

It had begun so innocently.

The Srivastava family enjoyed an illustrious heritage. Of the powerful Kayasth caste ranking on par with Brahmins, holding ample farmland that generated enough profit even to buy a Jeep, they were revered and respected throughout the region. But the Srivastavas weren't satisfied to enjoy their status. Long before Alok's birth, his grandfather Shri Bhaguti Srivastava had gained an education and learned to speak English in the days of the British East India Company before India's independence. Observing the lack of secondary education, he had donated a parcel of land to the government and on it founded a high school. He named it Sri Shankrachary Intercollege in honor of his favorite guru. The high school thrived and provided education to countless local children, its management passing eventually to Alok's father. Thus Alok grew up in an unusually educated environment, learning to speak English from an early age.

As far back as he could remember, Alok and his family faithfully ministered to the gods, trekking weekly along the packed mud pathways through the fields to the local temple. In his youth the stories of gods and goddesses had fascinated Alok. He yearned to be mighty and strong and shrewd like the gods in the legends. He also became acutely aware of his sinfulness. Through the guidance of religious leaders and the pervading traditions, Alok decided the sure pathway to attaining both power and pardon from sin entailed becoming a devotee of the deity whose dominion exceeded all the gods.

Some of Destroyer's disciples emulate his ascetic life by begging, fasting and substituting cremation ashes for clothing. But Alok chose another way to follow and please his god. Known as "lord of bhang," Destroyer loves both smoking and imbibing psychedelics and is pleased when his devotees join him for a high. Initially with the intent of gaining spiritual power and relief from the guilt of sin, Alok began to worship Destroyer not with the traditional offerings of milk and incense, but by smoking marijuana and drinking *bhang lassi*.

But as his worship deteriorated into addiction, alcohol was added to the menu. His search of finances to nourish his cravings led him into drug dealing and demoted his reputation from respected middle son of the high school principal to being numbered among the dregs of human indignity.

In Hindu culture, when one family member is wayward, the whole family is shamed and humiliated and loses respect in the community. So the waywardness of the black sheep son inflicted extreme duress upon his parents and siblings. His father and mother undertook great efforts to help their son. They called in the doctors and sorcerers and the priests. They took Alok to the temples, where gurus and god-men chanted mantras, cast spells over him and attempted to exorcize his demons—to no avail. Alok continued to drink, steal and do drugs.

"Why can't you be a good man? You bring shame on our family." But if they were goaded by shame, Alok was being gouged by it. He could no longer endure the shame of causing his family shame. The decision he had pondered for weeks had now been made; he would leave home and not return. Heartsick from causing his family sorrow, Alok wrote a note admonishing them not to grieve for him. He would no longer bring them sorrow, because they would not see him again. Upon leaving the house, he snatched up the family's VCR—a rare and costly item in those days, affordable only to the upper middle class—and set off for a distant city.

One of Alok's few remaining friends worked at a warehouse on the highway in the outskirts of town. When Alok appealed to him for a place to lay his head, the friend offered him what accommodation was available. The single amenity elevating the eight-by-eight concrete box from par with a military bunker was a barred window encrusted with spiderwebs and dust. A hard cot and a plastic table with a broken leg completed the furnishings.

Alok sold the VCR to buy alcohol and drugs. Utter darkness and hopelessness overcame him. His existence degenerated into a swirling sea of dread. *I have no one in the world. I have left my family and pledged not to return. My friend won't put up with me living here much longer. Where will I go? What is the point? What future do I have?*

For such tormentous questions the liquor shop provided a ready escape. But this time a few shots failed to drown his pain. Then a deep horror swooped over him, a shadow enclosing him, suffocating him. With a force of compulsion arising from a dark, nonmaterial source, he heard himself blurt out, "My future doesn't matter because I don't have a future. I won't leave this place. I will die here. I will commit suicide. I will die. I must die. I don't deserve to live." Claws had grabbed him. The darkness was taking him down, down into oblivion. Death. What was death like? From childhood he had feared death.

A scene began to play before his eyes. His grandfather's funeral. Saucer-eyed with horror and revulsion, the six-year-old watched the flames eating away the flesh of the gentle old man who had taken him on his knee and fed him *golis* made from milk and sugar. When the sight of the cremation was too much, he had screamed and run away, unable to bear the terror. His mother had brought him back to the pyre, though allowing him to stand behind her and hide his face in her *sari*.

After it was over, he had asked his father, "Where do we go after we die?" But his father could not provide an answer. So Alok had lived his whole life wondering, fearing, dreading that terrifying end called death. That is another reason he worshiped Destroyer, whom, attested the legends, held the power of death and the afterlife.

Alok lifted his tearstained face from his hands. "But I don't want to die," he cried. "I want to stop being afraid and stop causing people to be sad. I long to be a good man."

Then one last glimmer of hope flittered on his conscience. He remembered the early days, the grandiose legends extolling Destroyer's power and might. It had to be true. It must be real. Surely his god could hear. Why hadn't he answered? Why hadn't he delivered him from the clutches of addiction? *Perhaps*, thought Alok, *I haven't prayed hard enough. Maybe I haven't done enough penance. I haven't proven my devotion and my god is waiting for a genuine act of reverence.*

With that Alok arose from the log on which he was sitting next to the open-front liquor store. Down the road a few hundred feet stood a bookshop—a four-wheeled cart four feet long with an upright affixed to one side. Piled up on the cart were books and magazines, everything from the *Guinness Book of World Records* to *Time* magazine. Staggering up to the bookshop, Alok requested the publication likely to be the last printed material he would ever read, and which constituted his terminal strand of hope. The paperback booklet with glossy cover featured a blue cross-legged figure lost in meditation. Inside were countless mantras of worship and praise to Destroyer.

Trudging back to his room, Alok's heart cried out to the only hope of deliverance he knew, the god he had all his life believed could help him. Gripping the book of mantras, he swore, "I will chant mantras and pray day and night for two days. If my god doesn't answer me or deliver me from this darkness, then on the morning of the third day I will die. I will go and lie on the railroad track and commit suicide."

Stocking an ample supply of pot, Alok locked himself in the room and began to chant. From the depths of his heart and the annals of his ragged soul, he cried out to Destroyer, singing his praises and beseeching him for mercy. Prostrating himself on the grimy concrete floor, he wept pools of tears begging his god to answer him, to show himself, to reveal himself and rescue him from his hopeless state of addiction.

Sweating profusely, trembling with effort, Alok at last fell mute. Listening. Straining his last sinew of spiritual aptitude into the unseen realm, waiting—for what? Anything. Optimally a voice or a vision or a visitation from a heavenly being. But even to be graced by a slight sense of his god's presence near him would be sufficient, any miniscule sign that his god was listening, had heard, some clue that he cared. But the only aura that invaded the room's empty solitude was routine, humdrum India—horns honking, a squeaky, semi-melodious *bhajan* drifting from a temple loudspeaker, the intermittent buzzing of a fly alighting on a bottle lip, and the indomitable, all-penetrating sticky heat.

"Speak to me! Speak to me!" His scream banged against the gray concrete walls and returned into his own mouth, wasted.

Then he heard the train. The long, piercing whistle announced its arrival from afar. Faintly at first but growing, growing, the engine's roar and the wheels on the tracks and great iron couplers linking the bogies. Horror gripped him. The train. The railroad tracks. Scarcely one more day. A few hundred yards, a few moments' walk, and he would be standing on those steel rails.

He saw himself there. To his right the tracks curved, skirting the police quarters and an apartment complex. The trains took this curve fast and only slowed upon reaching the straight span from the curve to the station. Far to his left the track split into four and between each rose a concrete platform. Beyond lay the station where the trains halted to embark and disembark their passengers and cargo. Stairways rose from each platform to an elevated walkway on which passengers crossed from one platform to the other above the trains. Cluttering the tracks along the station were discarded half-eaten *samosas*, banana peels, plastic wrappers and a generous supply of human and mammalian excrement putrefying in sewer water, throughout which obese rats merrily foraged and fought.

Alok had chosen this place beyond the turn for a reason; the conductor wouldn't have time to slow the juggernaut that must end his life. The tracks beneath his feet were black and rusted where the tie plate and spikes cinched them to the wooden beam one-third buried in gravel. But the upper surface of the track that bore the pressure of the train wheels had been polished to a high sheen, gray-white steel gleaming in the sun.

Not for long.

He saw himself stretching his body across the iron rails. His last offering, laid not before his god, who had deceived him, but now laid before a train, to be slaughtered by cold steel and soot. One rail beneath his neck. Severed head. This should ensure a quick death. His heart, still alive, would pump his blood out to cover the tracks. So much for shiny smooth steel. A feast for the packs of half-starved mongrels.

215

Staring up at the harsh blue-gray sky, the sun scorched his face one last time. The train whistle from afar pierced his ears. He flinched at its prick. Only a few more seconds.

Then a sensation truly terrifying that he hadn't counted on—through the molecules of iron beneath his neck rose the tremors of the approaching train, transmitted domino-effect through the length of the track. The rumbling roar that would end his life reached his skin before it reached his ears. Louder, stronger, vibrating his neck like an electric razor. He dared not turn his head to look.

Then the tortured scream of steel sliding on steel. From the corner of the one eye that he dared to open, he saw fiery sparks flying from the wheels. Glimpsing the wretched figure on the tracks, the conductor had activated all brakes in a desperate attempt to halt the careening behemoth.

I'm sorry, Alok thought. *One more person I have hurt. I'm sorry, conductor. You are the last. Now my worthless life is over. I won't hurt anyone else.*

Wheels locked, the multi-ton locomotive continued to slide forward with minimally abated velocity. For an instant Alok thought, *What if instead of rolling over me the locked wheels push me along the track and slowly crush me?* Horror seethed through his body. Everything in him screamed, *Get up! Get off the track!* But he resisted, fingers clawing into the gravel.

Above the din of steel-on-steel, the conductor's voice shrieked, "Get off the track! Get off the track!" his arm waving wildly, torso leaning out the window.

Alok jerked back into himself. The cot. The marijuana leaves. A half-smoked joint smoldering on the floor. The gloomy room. Cold, wet skin, shirt sticking to his back. Heart pounding. He was still alive. But for how long? One

216

day left. The pounding of his heart throbbed in his ears, ominous, the ticking of a bomb. Only so many more beats, each one carrying him relentlessly toward oblivion. The end. But what awaited him on the other side of death? The thought terrified him beyond the far limits of dread, and he thrust it away as if it were a fanged beast.

The mantra book had fallen open facedown on the floor. Horrified, he snatched it up. By thus disgracing his god, he could have undone an entire day's worth of prayer.

"You must speak to me," he cried. "I don't want to die. Please, I don't want to die. But if you do not speak to me, I am dead already. I cannot go on in these chains."

Another day passed in relentless prayer interspersed with visits to the roadside bottle shop and the narcotics hawkers who, swiftly recognizing one of their own, provided ample supply of irresistible weed.

But still his god was silent. No vision. No voice. No deliverance. No hope. Late into the night Alok prayed and cried, cried and prayed. No answer. At last, exhausted, inebriated and frustrated, Alok screamed, "There is no god. No hope exists for me. Tomorrow I must die. Tomorrow when the train comes I must die." Then he fell into a stuporous and fitful, drugged sleep.

"Alok! Alok, get up!"

He rolled over on the cot, half-awake, groggy. Had he heard a voice? Had someone called his name?

"Alok! It's late. Get up."

An audible voice!

Alok leaped out of bed trembling, looking this way and that for the source of the command. But no one was in the room.

"Who . . . who's there?" his voice quavered.

No answer.

But now he was certain that a living presence had addressed him. Terror gripped him. What if a ghost had spoken to him? What if he was losing his mind?

Desperate to escape the eerie atmosphere and surround himself with people, Alok bolted from the room. His feet carried him unsteadily down the pathway toward the highway. It seemed to take ages to reach the familiar bottle shop beneath a spreading banyan. There, along the highway, morning as usual was in full swing. The *chai wallah* busily poured tea from a great aluminum pot and flipped *jalebi* frying in a cauldron of smoking grease. Customers stood helter-skelter, sipping their chai from thick-walled glasses while others streamed in and out of the general store buying biscuits and little plastic bags of milk. A lumbering herd of buffalo plodded past en route to grazing, trailed by a boy waving a stick.

At the edge of the road he drew up short, heaving. His feet were rooted to the ground. For a long moment he stood staring across the road, not seeing, mind reeling. The voice still echoed. If it was a ghost, at least he had escaped. He had fled from its presence and now he was safe.

Or was it a ghost? Or a god? An audible voice had called his name, of this he was certain. The voice emanated not from a human, because not a soul had passed into or near the room.

"God. God called my name." It began to register. "Maybe it wasn't a ghost. Maybe it was a god. Maybe some god out there cares for me."

But what god? Was it Destroyer? Or perhaps another member of the pantheon had been moved with compassion for this wretched earthling.

He reasoned with himself, collecting his wits and settling his racing adrenaline. Meanwhile his eyes stared blankly, foggily, at the goings-on across the highway.

Then his vision cleared and he comprehended what his eyes were seeing.

There, opposite from the bottle shop, stood a new building. People were arriving on cycles and on foot and going in through the open doorway. The previous day he had vaguely observed a painter up on a scaffold. In bright red paint he was writing words over the entrance, but Alok hadn't paid him much heed. Now the writing was complete. It read, *The wages of sin is death, but the gift of God is eternal life through Jesus Christ our Lord. Romans 6:23.*

Alok squinted, trying to remember. . . . He'd heard a story long ago as a child—something about a god called Jesus. He was told that Jesus was the god of the British. His book, the Bible, was the British religious book, so no good Hindu should ever read it or attend one of their religious services. But the moment this flitted into his memory, it was repulsed by a cry of desperation.

This is my last day! This is the morning when I end my life! From this place I must go to the railroad tracks. I must die in a few minutes, he thought. *This verse says the wages of sin is death. That's right. I am a sinner. I deserve to die. If no god can help me, I am going to die.* Impulsively he rubbed his neck, cringing from the terror of the train bearing down on him, the vibrating track. . . .

But, he reasoned, *this verse also says, "The gift of God is eternal life." Can this God give me life? Could the voice I heard have been the voice of this God, calling my name?*

Then the unexplainable happened. Though no people were near, a force pushed him from behind. As if by a giant hand placed on his shoulders, he was thrust forward into the highway. Oblivious to what vehicles might be coming, he found his feet carrying him across the road. As he stumbled forward, a form, horrible and black, spiraled out of his body, a giant shadow peeling off of his shoulders and flying away.

Then his feet stood below the entrance. Directly above his head the words of hope shone with new red paint. *". . . the gift of God is eternal life."* Through whom? Not Destroyer. *". . . through Jesus Christ."*

Self-conscious of his sweaty, dismally bedraggled condition, Alok timidly entered the building. A cheery-faced person greeted him with a hearty handshake, unheedful of Alok's outward appearance. He proffered a glass of water, which Alok thankfully drained. Then, with a friendly hand on his shoulders, the man helped him to a seat near the front.

The preacher began to expound the meaning of Romans 6:23. Alok's ears imbibed the life-giving message of a God who so loved the world as to personally come and live among us, who suffered the penalty of our sin and set us free from the fear of death. Hope sprang alive in his heart when he learned that this God overcame death, rising again from the grave. He is the Living God who exacts no penance and imposes no rituals, but who truly hears and answers prayer.

That day, instead of lying on the railroad track, Alok knelt at the altar and received Jesus into his heart. He was liberated from the chains of death and fear and sin that had beset him, and completely delivered from his addictions. From that day he began a brand-new life, full of the glory and power and victory he had so desperately sought. A treasure chained in darkness had been freed.

When Alok returned to his family, at first his father objected to his newfound faith. When he told them what had happened to him, they drove him from the village shouting, "You have left the family traditions! You have abandoned our gods!" His father cried, "You are no longer my son!"

This season of persecution was God's plan, because Alok found refuge with the pastor of the church where he had been delivered, and was mentored under his leadership. Passionate to love, follow and serve his one-and-only Lord, King and God with every ounce of his being, Alok developed into a flaming evangelist, sharing his redemption story with anyone who would listen.

He also kept on loving and returning to his family, waiting for them to accept him. Soon Alok's father observed that his son no longer cursed, drank or used or sold drugs. His former demeanor of gloom had transformed into a glowing joy and confidence. Instead of carousing and running with the gangs, Alok now sat for hours reading the Bible and boldly sharing his transformation story with his former gang friends, of whom several joined him in the adventure of relationship with "the Living God." Chatter and questions and whispers arose throughout the village. What strange power, the people asked their comrades, had instigated this astounding metamorphosis of the "Srivastava black sheep"? The answer, which they at last had to acknowledge, was, "Jesus Christ."

One grand, triumphal day, his father declared, "I do not fully understand what happened to you, son, but it's marvelous. I am proud to call you my son. You have become a good man!"

In the year 2003 TellAsia's work under David's leadership was thriving, and the organization was growing both in the United States and India. I knew it was time to add a new region. But how could we expand without another qualified native leader? I began to pray, *Lord, please give us another David.* I had told David, "I am praying for God to clone you."

God did not clone David, but He did answer my prayer by bringing to me another exceptional native-general to lead the charge in a new region.

A conference was held in Delhi to discuss ideas for reaching the vast and populous northern area. As an international agency leader, I had been invited. This puzzled me, since those most essential to a practical and fruitful action plan were not internationals but the natives. Since David was just such a genuine indigenous native of the epicenter of the specific area under discussion, I took liberty to bring him along.

Arriving at the meeting, I assessed the participants. Hardly a single native of north India was in attendance of this meeting in which they, the few precious native believers, ought to have been not just present but the guests of honor. Men from America and England represented corporations and foundations. Indian missionaries from more evangelized regions swarmed around them trying to give them their packets of information or show their PowerPoint presentations on their laptops, in hopes of securing financial support. But not a single native did I see, except my David.

But I was wrong.

There was another native in the room. Unrecognized and unheeded by the Indian missionaries and the suited corporation heads and project directors, a young man looked on with downhearted longing. He had no fancy suit to wear, and outwardly he appeared insignificant, but inside he knew he was a king, commissioned by the King to rescue his kinsmen. He knew no fancy phrases to describe his vision for serving his people, but his personal experience of radical deliverance far exceeded technical words. He was a living representative of millions searching for hope and light. Though wanting in English eloquence, his fluency in the local dialect enabled his words to penetrate straight to the hearts of his fellow villagers. He possessed no laptop computer and no concept of how to make a presentation. But within his soul drummed the heartbeat of his beloved country, along with the divine mandate to bring them the glorious "gift of God" that he himself had so dramatically received.

When, with anxiety and sweating palms, he ventured to strike up a conversation with an American or Englishman, he was dismayed to discover that they found his broken English difficult to follow. Thus deeming him a minor- and not a major-league player, they discreetly excused themselves after a brief interchange and moved on to others. Intent on nabbing a few minutes with a Westerner or dismissing him for his obvious youth, the missionaries pushed past him with no greater salute than would have been granted the janitor or sweeper.

The meeting was called to order and proceeded with designated speakers casting grand propositions for how to bring salvation, education and hope to the masses. Alok watched in awe while a high-tech projector beamed great maps of his homeland up on the overhead screen. The maps depicted precisely the villages and towns where he had preached and led hundreds to Christ.

But no one invited him to comment.

Sitting near the back of the auditorium and gazing across the participants, he noticed a peculiarity—something that jolted his heart into a faster rhythm and captured his full attention.

A few rows ahead sat a fellow native of north India, David. They had met once, and had rejoiced in finding common ground—two educated middle-class youths who had encountered Jesus and were now, by no one's order but His, ambassadors of His deliverance to their countrymen. Many years had passed since they had met, but now David's physique appeared healthier than before, his face radiating enthusiasm. But it wasn't so much David that caught Alok's attention, as who was beside him.

To his left sat a young American woman, and now and then they whispered to one another or exchanged a paper as if in close partnership. Alok stared with wondering curiosity. *One of the internationals is paying attention to us natives?* he thought. *This must be an unusual person, to overlook our lack of gray hairs and our shabby attire and our imperfect English.*

After the session Alok introduced himself to me, and I knew he was the answer to my prayers for a second key leader of TellAsia's work in India. According to my custom, by the Lord's direction I asked Alok to tell me how he envisaged delivering his people from bondage. I was thrilled to learn that he shared my assignment of training and mobilizing the native people to serve their own communities regardless of organizational affiliation. He shared my God-sized visions, believing large-scale transformation across north India to be a reachable goal. Thus we birthed an initiative that, as of the penning of this book, has resulted in hundreds of thousands of lives set free from fear, bondage and poverty.

Because of Alok's dramatic salvation and our teamwork together through TellAsia Ministries, thousands searching for meaning, hopeless addicts broken and ashamed, outcastes and drug addicts and thieves, have been delivered from the claws of death and fear and given a new future. Picking up the mantle of his grandfather, Alok founded a primary school providing top-quality English education at a price affordable even to the Dalit villagers. A few years later, election time rolled around. Recognizing that Alok had become a man of honesty, compassion and wisdom, the same community amongst which he once sold drugs elected him Pradhan, chief of fourteen villages. Not only had Jesus made Alok a "good man," He had made him a true prince and an ambassador of God's will for social equality, economic stability and spiritual liberation.

Throughout those early days of TellAsia's work in India, I remained only vaguely aware of the risks and needs of the children of this region. However, one day the Lord spoke to me. With resounding clarity on par with the day He had summoned me to "start in India," He said, *The most Christlike act a person can do in this life is to give Jesus and a bright future to a child who has no hope."*

Soon afterward I discovered that Alok's wife, Ricky, had herself grown up in a children's home deep in the Himalayas. Through her own situation she had received a vision to help other children in desperate situations. Thus in 2005 TellAsia launched Blue Haven Children's Home, a loving sanctuary for orphaned, semi-orphaned, abused and destitute children.

Funding for our church planting and training of leaders had been provided in reasonable proficiency. Due to the large numbers of people coming to Christ and the rapid multiplication of our house-based church groups, TellAsia had received international recognition. Our strategies and the dedication and fruitfulness of our native leaders had drawn respect. My invested efforts of traveling, speaking in churches and presenting grant proposals paid off in resources necessary to continue growing the work.

Thus, upon receiving the Lord's commission to rescue and educate children, I set out likewise to develop the funding necessary. Teachers must be trained and paid. Homes must be built to house children. Schools must be built to educate them. Rural parents must be taught how to identify and avoid traffickers. With thirty million such children in desperate need and hardly a single agency or Christ-centered group intervening, it seemed that supporters would flock to help. This compelling opportunity to invade such deep darkness with the light of love, nurture and education should have been an easy sell.

However, hours upon countless hours stretched into months and years of near-fruitless labor. We received only scant funds toward the cause. Our visions of rescuing hundreds of children had to be put on hold. I realized that I had come up against some of the warlords' most heavily fortified bulwarks. They were not able to keep our churches out of the villages, but they were dead-set on keeping their stranglehold on impoverished children. I at last concluded there must be one thing the powers of darkness deem most valuable to the maintenance of their oppressive reign, one type of human life that they want to destroy more than any other—

Children.

Because children are most precious to God, therefore they are most hated by the powers of darkness. More than anything in the world, those powers desire to prevent children from entering the liberty and joy of God's destiny for their lives. The powers of darkness fear children more than anyone else, because they are the future of nations. If the children can be lifted out of poverty, illiteracy and disgrace, the nation will follow.

But all around us swirled the chains of the warlords with no way to liberate their captives. Through these battles for the ragged treasures bound in brothels, malnutrition and death, the only stimulant that kept me going was the glowing faces of our few children in Blue Haven Home whom we were able to rescue and support. Our burgeoning team of native leaders stood ready and waiting to be mobilized. But without start-up funds or buildings, our ability to reach the hapless and hopeless with life and deliverance remained miniscule compared to the need.

And as we labored and prayed and did what we could, a tragedy and a triumph unfolded. . . .

The Missing Face

"Pooja! Wake up. Get yourself out of that bed." Fingers cracked and calloused delivered a shove to the shoulder beneath the tattered blanket. "Lazy girl. Do I have to rouse you every morning? Can't you remember your duties and wake up on time?"

Brittle and yellow-tinged from malnutrition, her tangled locks stuck out from her head in every direction as she sat up. Rubbing her eyes with fists yet grimy from digging roots last night, she was still clad in her mud-colored school dress with broken belt. *I just slept a few hours. Is it morning already?* wondered Pooja. But the wizened mother had already turned and limped off to start the morning fire.

The blue light of early dawn filtered coldly through tears in the rag covering a square porthole in the mud wall. A chill January gust bit through Pooja's thin garment. The only clothing she had to fend off the winter freeze, a threadbare shawl, had been applied atop the thin blanket for a tiny bit of precious added insulation throughout the night. Shivering, she snatched it up with desperation and wrapped it around her shoulders.

The few steps on the icy floor from cot to shoes sent jabs of pain up her legs. Black nylon socks having long ago given way to gaping holes, she pulled them on, then turned them bottoms-up, so at least her toes and heels would have a few threads between them and the hard soles of her shoes.

The shawl had fallen onto the floor. Immediately chilled again, she feverishly flipped it back on and jammed her feet into the scuffed black shoes. The laces had long since broken and been cast away. They weren't needed anyway, since she had outgrown the shoes two years ago.

Outside, Diva was popping buffalo-dung patties off the wall of the hut where she had slapped them several days ago to dry. Her rasping cough at every fifth breath informed Pooja that Mother was still ill and might not be able to work in the field again today. *At least we have the buffalo,* she thought. *So long as we have fuel and milk we can survive.*

Diva was shoving the reed basket and long, curved blade into Pooja's hands. "Get along, hurry," she muttered through a cough. "Minju is hungry and Baby spilled his water bucket."

The fog hung low and dense over the misty green fields, and the weeds and blades of grass bowed across the path with a load of dripping water. They left their generous deposit as Pooja's legs brushed past. By the time she reached the grassy area where the villagers gathered fodder for their animals, she was drenched from the waist down. A knot formed in her stomach while she worked laying fistful after fistful of long green stems across the basket. The knot subsided in a hungry growl. *I wonder if we'll have breakfast,* she thought. Not a day passed that she didn't fear starvation. She couldn't remember the last time she'd had three meals in one day. She envied the buffalo. They never went hungry. *I would be so happy,* she thought, *if there was someone who cared for me like Mother and I care for Minju.*

At last Pooja hoisted the basket of grass onto her head and set out for home. What she could carry would satisfy Minju's huge mouth and stomach for a few hours. Mother would have to come and cut grass again at midday, but this early morning breakfast, insisted Mother, kept the milk flowing.

After pouring out the grass for Minju and her calf, Pooja assessed the water situation. Minju's bucket was half-empty, and the calf had spilled his. Pooja glared at the calf, who stared back with dumb, glassy eyes.

"You stupid," she muttered. "Don't you know how hard it is to bring you water?"

Extracting the calf's bucket from the mud, she set off, her shoes clacking and tripping on the irregular bricks stuck into the clay to create a primitive roadway through the middle of the village. Hugging the roadside with a few feet of space to spare were the huts of her fellow villagers. Like her mother, women were fanning wood and cow-dung fires into flame. But unlike her mother, they were also sorting pebbles from rice and preparing *roti* dough and chopping into pieces green gourds and yellow pumpkins and green okra and greener spinach. Pooja's mouth watered at the thought of a real hot breakfast of *roti* and such delectable vegetables. She could hardly remember the last time she had such a meal. The best her mother could provide was rice and *daal.*

She couldn't help but notice that the huts she passed were in better condition than hers, whose bamboo roof was rotted and falling in and the walls eroded from the summer rains. "You must repair your walls," she had overheard a neighbor saying to her mother. "Or your hut will collapse with the monsoon and you will be killed."

But her mother had no money or strength to repair the hut, and the villagers expressed no pity. Even blood relatives considered them outcastes. "Your mother is cursed woman," an aunt had once whispered to Pooja. "When husband die, it means the gods have judged that wife is unworthy of husband and handed her over to devils."

Pooja was not sure she believed this, but it scared her. Was her mother really a bad woman? Did that mean she, Pooja, was also a bad girl? Had she and her mother truly been handed over to the devils? These fears and questions piled on top of her fear of starvation, steeping her tender mind in turmoil.

"Psst! Come here!"

From the dwindling shadows emerged another little girl.

Pooja's grim face brightened at the sight of her only friend. Neha's family had moved to the village and apparently hadn't yet heard the rumors surrounding Pooja's recently deceased father. Either that, or for some inexplicable reason they didn't fear the devils, because Neha befriended Pooja while the other kids kept their distance.

Mindful to stay on task despite her longing to stop and be a normal little girl, Pooja set her bucket under the spout and began pumping. After several strokes of the long, steel handle, water began to dribble out into the bucket.

"Did you study for the exam?" asked Neha.

"When can I study?" moaned Pooja. "All I ever have time to do is work. Mother is alone and sick. I have no older brother. No papa. What to do?"

"Not to worry." Neha touched her friend tenderly on the shoulder. "I'll help you rehearse on our way to school."

Pooja brightened momentarily and managed a smile as she hefted the half-full water bucket and set off back toward her hut. But just as quickly her face darkened again. She longed to study and to become an educated girl. More than fun and play or enjoyment, she dreamed of having a job someday.

"Study hard in school," her mother had charged, "because education is the pathway to a happy life. Educated people aren't hungry. They have vegetables and *roti* and even sweets. They have brick houses with real roofs, and they even have electricity."

Thus Pooja's dream, and her mother's dream for her, was to go to school and learn to read and write. Then someday she could marry a good educated husband, and maybe even get a job.

But she couldn't concentrate on school. Instead, hunger kept jerking her mind back to her mother's fire and the paramount question—whether there would be any nourishment cooking there besides watery tea with a dribble of Minju's precious milk.

Neha's mother raked a near-toothless comb through her hair, making her wince, and deftly tied the belt of her mud-brown school dress. "Are you ready for the exam?"

"Yes, Mother."

The mother took Neha's face in her hands. "Look straight at me. Both eyes."

But try as she might, only Neha's right eye could look straight ahead. Her left eye rolled uncontrollably to the side, giving her a comical look.

Her mother placed a hand over her right eye. "Can you see me?"

"No. I see the wall."

"Please, baby, try to see me," she pleaded.

"I'm trying, but I can't," moaned Neha. "My eye won't go straight."

The mother stood with a hopeless sigh. The doctor's words haunted her: "Unless you have your daughter's eye corrected, she'll go blind before she's twenty." But the operation cost over twenty thousand rupees, or three hundred dollars—more than the family's entire annual income.

The mother forced a smile. "You must study well and become a good educated girl. Then you won't be poor and oppressed like your mom and dad."

"Yes, Mother," replied Neha. "I will be a teacher and help other poor children become smart and happy."

"Very good. You can be a teacher, but you must do well in your classes. Now, eat your breakfast."

Neha's mother pressed a tiny bowl of wheat porridge and a cup of black tea into hers and her brother Inder's hands, then turned abruptly back to the fire to flip a *roti*.

The children held their meager victuals, somber gazes wordlessly grieving that there was no porridge left for Mother. This was a lean day. When there wasn't enough for everyone to at least have a little, and not even a few peas in the porridge or a dribble of milk in the tea, it meant times were hard. Perhaps Papa hadn't found a landowner to hire him to harvest his field. Perhaps it was time to pay the rent, or some other unforeseen expense had arisen and consumed the tiny remnant of money available for food.

"Eat," urged their mother without turning from her fire. "You can't study on an empty stomach."

Into each little plastic tiffin box she placed one precious *roti* and a sprinkling of salt—a lunch for which they were deeply grateful.

After their scant breakfast, the children donned their book bags and set out for the only school their parents could afford. Their mother watched their receding backs and shook her head. Typical of rural government-run schools, the teachers were known for being late, absent, abusive toward certain children and preferential of others and occasionally even drunk. Though Neha and Inder studied hard, they weren't learning much. The teacher's instruction confused them, while she and their father, being illiterate, were helpless to provide tutoring. How she longed to send her children to one of the grand private schools where the teachers cared for their students and taught them English and where they might even learn about that unfathomable piece of intimidating technology—the computer.

One hope existed by which such a miracle might befall her family—God. After the children were out of sight, she unwrapped from a plastic vegetable bag the only new item the family had owned in years and by far the most precious—a Bible. She couldn't read it, but she hoped that one day her children could.

Pressing it to her breast, she prayed, "Lord Jesus, I don't know You very well yet. I am like a newborn baby. But I believe You are the Living God who answers prayer. Pastor Kamal taught that the Bible says if we ask we will receive and if we knock we won't be turned away. So I'm asking You, please, please don't let my daughter go blind, and make a way for my children to have good nutritious food to eat and a good education. Let my children not have to go hungry to feed their children, and let them be able to read Your book to us."

At the edge of the village, brother and sister parted company. Inder rendezvoused with a group of his classmates while Neha hung back waiting for Pooja. "Don't be late," Inder

shouted back over his shoulder. "Teacher will thrash you."
But in a few moments Pooja appeared, hurrying through the
fields toward her friend.

Hair still uncombed and scraggly, brown dress besmudged
with traces of buffalo dung, she pantingly joined Neha, and
the two seven-year-olds began their trek toward the bigger
village and their school.

"You look tired," noted Neha apologetically.

"Why not?" moaned Pooja. "I've been working since four
a.m."

"Did you eat any food?"

"No. Did you?"

"A little. Didn't you even get some rice?"

"No. We don't have any rice."

"Well, at least I bet you had milk in your tea. You're lucky
you have a buffalo. We don't have a buffalo."

Pooja trudged along, head bowed. "A dribble of milk is
all." Pooja wiped a tear and sniffed hard. "My stomach hurts.
I feel sick."

"Here." Neha stopped and set her book bag on the ground.
Its zipper broken, a single safety pin in the top precariously
kept the books from tumbling out. She reached in and withdrew the tiffin, warm from the fresh *roti* inside. "Eat this."

Pooja stared at her, incredulous.

"I mean it." Neha's one good eye smiled invitingly to her
friend as she thrust the box into her hands. "Take it."

Tears flooding her eyes, Pooja took the box as if it contained fragile jewels, reverently opened it and bit into the *roti*.

After a few swallows, Pooja reminisced, "You were going
to help me review for the test today."

"Oh," sighed Neha. "I thought I knew how to do the math
problems, but I don't understand. Adding double numbers,

I mean. Teacher didn't explain how to do it. When I add 25 and 25 I get 410, and that can't be right. Also I have memorized the alphabet, but I don't understand how the letters go together, how they form words."

"Well, maybe she will teach us today," offered Pooja. "Didn't you want to be a teacher when you grow up?"

"Yeah."

"You will be a good teacher, I know it."

Neha chuckled. "No! Why do you think I would be a good teacher?"

"You care and you help people. Besides, you're smart." Pooja savored the last bite of *roti* and sucked the traces of salt and oil from her fingers. "Do you know what I will become when I grow up?"

"No, what will you become?"

The grimness of Pooja's face had waned into joy, and her step had a bounce to it. Hope had returned with the warmth in her tummy. She dropped the empty tiffin box into the gap in Neha's book bag. "Guess!"

Neha crinkled her face, thinking. "Maybe . . . you want to be a nurse?"

Pooja wrinkled her nose and gave her head a deft shake, untrimmed hair swirling. "No, not a nurse. They have to do yucky work like wipe people's behinds."

After a hearty laugh, Neha tried again. "Then maybe you want to . . . work in an office and type on a computer?"

Again Pooja shook her head. "Naw. That sounds boring. Guess again!"

"I give up," sighed Neha. "Come on, tell me."

"I will become an air hostess!" Pooja spread her arms and ran ahead, mimicking takeoff, book bag bouncing on her back and hair streaming in the wind. "I will fly high in the sky and serve so much lovely food to famous people going to faraway places and hear their stories. Maybe one day I will be famous, too. Maybe I will be a movie star!"

Neha snickered. "Wild dreams! But first, you know, we have to get an education."

"I want so desperately to learn," admitted Pooja, "but letters and numbers are so hard, so confusing. Do air hostesses have to know how to read and write and do math? They just have to look beautiful and serve food and tell people not to be afraid of the plane crashing."

Neha made a face. "I'm sure they have to be able to read and do math. Otherwise how would they know what food to serve or how many meals to prepare?"

Pooja was unstymied. "But really. Don't you think I could be a movie star?" She pawed at her hair and attempted to assume the pose of the female heroine on a poster advertising a recent Bollywood flick.

"Maybe." Neha shrugged. "But I don't have a chance with my eye sideways. I'm ugly. At least your face is nice to look at."

"You're not ugly," protested Pooja. "You're very pretty. I don't even notice your eye. Besides, you have a papa who cares for you. My papa was mean to me and then he died."

"I hardly see my papa," noted Neha. "From morning to night he works in the field to try to give us food to eat. At least your mama has a house and a buffalo. Our money goes for rent and nothing is left over. But," continued Neha, "that is why we must study. Life will not improve for us unless we learn to read and write. Let us go together and ask Teacher to explain the letters and the math to us, okay?"

A commotion outside aroused Diva from sleep. She had tried to go out in the field and work, but she had swooned with dizziness. So faint she could barely drag herself back to the hut, she had collapsed on the cot and conked out.

Now, at the sudden awareness that she had visitors, sheer adrenaline propelled her onto her feet. Nobody ever visited her rickety hovel and the villagers shunned her, so this couldn't be good.

Hastily adjusting her *sari* and stepping into her *chappals* she ducked through the low doorway into the afternoon sunlight.

Before her stood three ladies whom she knew at once were not from her village—or from any village. Their bright new *saris* and manicured faces attested to apparent affluence. They wore thick mascara like movie stars, and their purses and shoes matched their dresses. They exuded an air of glamour that intimidated Diva. She resisted an urge to retreat back inside her hut and close the door.

"*Namaste*, Mrs. Kumar." The older of the three pressed her hands together in the traditional Indian greeting. Her *sari* sparkled with what Diva supposed might be diadems. "My name is Kendra." She smiled around at the others. "But everyone calls me Grandma."

Diva briefly returned the greeting.

"We apologize, it appears we have intruded upon your nap. You will pardon us."

"Oh no. No problem," stammered Diva. "I . . . I'm happy to meet you."

"Well, Mrs. Kumar," continued Grandma, "please allow us to introduce ourselves. We are with Dream Catcher School in Delhi. Dream Catcher is an all-female institution offering enrollment to a few lucky little girls." From her purse she

237

whisked a brightly printed brochure and placed it in Diva's wondering hands. Diva had never seen a piece of paper so shiny. She stared amazed at the cheery pictures of happy, well-fed children studying colorful books and the great arched entrance to the manicured campus. The grand four-story school building, windows trimmed in bright red, was so white and bright that it glowed. "Like heaven," mused Diva to herself.

"I am the head mistress of the school," declared Grandma, "and these fine ladies"—she gestured to her comrades—"are a few of the teachers."

Then to Diva's awe, Grandma spoke to the other ladies in a language she didn't understand, but which she immediately knew must be English.

In response one lady with a bright green *sari* stepped forward and said in English, "Hello, Mrs. Kumar, my name is Priyanka. Excuse me, you are most welcome."

The other joined her. "Good afternoon, Mrs. Kumar, my name is Jinku, and it is my sincere pleasure to have your honorable acquaintance, sir."

Diva was speechless, awed at the incredible knowledge of these teachers and unable to believe that fate had brought them all the way from Delhi to her remote village. She rubbed her eyes and looked again. No, she was not hallucinating. The ladies were still there.

"Mrs. Kumar, I can see you feel overwhelmed at your good fortune, but I'm sure you're a pious lady and the gods have had mercy on your suffering. Now, tell us about your dear Pooja. How old is she?"

"Wait," muttered Diva. "You must have come to the wrong place. Your school . . . surely is wonderful, but it must be expensive. See, I have no money." She made a helpless gesture toward the shabby hut. "My husband is dead and—"

"Oh, Mrs. Kumar!" Grandma chuckled and her chubby belly shook.

Diva could hardly keep from staring at it. *Grandma must be truly blessed,* thought Diva, *to have so much good food to eat.*

"Come!" Grandma beckoned. "Let us sit down."

Diva invited the ladies inside the hut, and they sat on the two cots since there were no chairs. Grandma continued, "We can see your sad plight, and we know that you have no money. But you must understand, we at Dream Catcher School try to help poor widows like you and children like your precious little Pooja. We have come to offer Pooja the education she longs for. The whole world will be open to her after she graduates from Dream Catcher School. Big hospitals will hire her to be a doctor or nurse. Big schools will ask her to teach. Airlines will invite her to be a flight attendant. . . . Why, she might even become a movie star! Imagine that, Mrs. Kumar—your little girl onstage before the world! You will no longer live in this hut. Pooja will make so much money she can buy you a real house in the city with tasty food and new clothes and even a maid."

Diva's mind whirled with joy overset by unanswered questions. Her untrained senses felt hopelessly buried beneath this onslaught of good fortune. From the confusion emerged a few cohesive questions. . . . How did these ladies learn of her whereabouts, and how did they know Pooja's name? How could Dream Catcher School pay the salaries of these classy teachers without charging fees from the students?

"Mrs. Kumar, look at this." Grandma pushed a document in front of her. "This is the admission form for your daughter to enroll in Dream Catcher School. You have only to place your thumbprint here." Her chubby finger pointed to a blank line at the bottom.

"But I can't read," protested Diva.

"Very well." Grandma smiled. "Madame Priyanka, would you read it for her?"

The lady in green took the paper and appeared to read: "I, Mrs. Diva Kumar of Chauraha village, hereby enroll and admit my daughter, Pooja Kumar, to Dream Catcher School. I understand that my daughter will be given an exam and placed in the level of education matching her age and abilities. Dream Catcher School will assume responsibility for Pooja's living expenses, including food, housing, medicine and education. . . ."

"But," asked Diva, "how can Dream Catcher School operate if you don't charge money from the parents?"

"Oh!" Grandma beamed a wide and proud smile. "Money is no problem for us. Wealthy businessmen from abroad provide the full support for Dream Catcher School. Parents have no financial burden."

"But I don't have money for bus fare. How can I bring Pooja to Delhi?"

"Nothing to worry about, Mrs. Kumar," tweedled Grandma. "Pooja can come along with us this very evening. We will take good care of her. In fact, first of all we'll take her to a restaurant and enjoy chicken curry together. Pooja will be happy with Grandma and her teachers, and she'll make lovely new friends."

Entirely disarmed, confused by a mixture of soaring hope darkened by a sense of foreboding that she pushed aside as unwarranted and faithless pessimism, Diva gave a sigh.

The green-swathed teacher held out the ink pad, smiling. A bit of her red lipstick had rubbed off on one of her front teeth.

Diva extended her leathery thumb. Grandma took it, pressed it onto the ink pad and then onto the paper. In another hour,

Pooja would be on her way to Dream Catcher School and a bright future . . . or so her mother hoped.

The optician's big fingers gently separated a ring of sticky surgical tape from the fine facial skin and lifted a gauze bandage from the eye. For a long moment he held the little girl's chin with one gloved hand. The other on her forehead, he tilted her head back and from side to side, bespectacled face inches from hers, assessing the progress. Then he placed a hand over her right eye. "Can you see me?"

"Yes. . . . Yes, I can see you!" exclaimed Neha.

Satisfied, he stepped back and addressed the woman seated across the room. "Mrs. Srivastava, everything is fine now. The operation was successful, and her eye has healed."

An attending nurse passed a hand mirror to Neha. A conglomerate of fear and excitement rose up in her heart. For the first time since the operation, she looked at her face and eye without the bandage. Then she gave a cry of joy. Both her eyes now looked straight ahead. She could see everything clearly.

The doctor scribbled a prescription on the hospital letterhead and handed the paper to Ricky. "She must stay on antibiotics a little longer. When the medicine is finished, bring her back for one final checkup."

"Thank you, Doctor." Ricky folded the prescription and took Neha's hand.

Face radiant, Neha exclaimed, "Thank you, Doctor!" and beaming up at Ricky, "Thank you, Auntie!"

When we started Blue Haven Children's Home we had announced to our village pastors, "If you come across an orphan or neglected child while traveling to the villages, let us know. The child may qualify for admittance to Blue Haven."

Word spread rapidly and when Pastor Kamal noticed one of his new believers with her unkempt and underfed children, he told us of Neha. Soon afterward we welcomed Neha as our eighth child in Blue Haven Children's Home.

A year after Neha joined Blue Haven, she received a phone call from her mother. Neha's mother could hardly fit a word in edgewise for the fountain of news that poured out of her daughter.

"Mother, you won't believe this," bubbled Neha. "Auntie Ricky fixed my eye! Here in the big city she took me to a good doctor and he did operation. Now my left eye doesn't look sideways anymore. I can see straight and everything is so bright and clear. I'm going to a good private school. The teachers come on time and they care for us and teach nicely so I understand my lessons. I learned to read and write, and now I can add, subtract and even multiply. I'm making A's in all my classes. I have lots of friends and I'm so happy!"

Her mother began to speak, but Neha, full of joy, kept talking.

"Oh, and Mother, I eat so much good food. There's not a day when I have to eat only *roti*. I get to eat three meals a day with vegetables and *daal*, and several times a week we eat eggs and even chicken and mutton. I have bright clothes now and shoes with laces and a trunk of my own to keep my clothes and a blue and pink patchwork quilt on my bed."

"How many other children live at Blue Haven?" queried Neha's mother.

"Thirty-two," chirped Neha. "We're like brothers and sisters, and we have so much fun together. One American lady also comes and teaches us. Her name is Leanna but we call her Sister Jyoti. She knows Hindi but she told us, 'If you are ready to talk to me, then come sit with me over here and

242

we will talk only English, no Hindi.' I was so scared because I didn't know English, but I thought to myself, *No, I won't be scared, I will learn English.* So four of us girls and a boy joined her class, and slowly I started to be able to talk English. Now, guess what, Mother. I am so confident. I can talk and talk in English, and even the rich kids in my school who have educated parents can't talk as much English as I can!"

"Amazing!" exclaimed Neha's mother. "Tell me more. What else are you learning?"

"Listen, Mother! I'm learning computer! At Blue Haven we have a computer and Sister Jyoti taught us how to put our fingers on the keys and how to use the mouse and make a Microsoft Word document and add pictures. Now I can even do email and internet."

"Do they teach you about Jesus?"

"Oh yes, we have devotional time daily. Auntie Ricky and Sister Jyoti and our house mother, Sister Einla, teach us the Bible, and we learn dances to Christian songs and skits that tell Bible stories. Mother, I believe it was because of Jesus that I came here to Blue Haven. He loves us and He is the living God and He hears our prayers."

"Yes." Neha's mother struggled to keep back tears of joy. "I know He hears our prayers. He heard mine. I'm so happy. Now my daughter has a bright future!"

"Mother," Neha continued. "Remember I told you I wanted to be a teacher? Now, because I am getting to study, I can become an excellent teacher. I will return to our village one day. I will teach the children in our village how to read and write and tell them about Jesus. Would you like that, Mother?"

Now her mother's joy was uncontrollable. "Yes, baby," she sobbed. "Now you can be a teacher, or anything else in the whole wide world that you wish to be!"

Neha's stream of good news paused. She had remembered her friend Pooja. Their last day together was vivid in her mind. Pushing aside all troubles, they had dreamed of a bright future. Neha hadn't realized that evening when they parted to go to their homes, it would be the last time she would see Pooja. The following morning Neha had waited and waited at the village edge, but Pooja didn't arrive. Later she found out that Pooja had gone to a fancy school far away.

"Mother," said Neha, "have you heard from Pooja? Does she like it there in Dream Catcher School? Is she also learning reading and writing and English and dances and computers? Is she happy?"

On the other end of the line, there was a long hesitation. Neha's mother searched for words. Neha knew something was wrong, and her face darkened. "Mother? Is Pooja okay?"

"No, baby." Her mother's voice was heavy with sorrow. "Pooja is dead."

Poor Diva had taken the thick makeup of the "teachers" as a sign of wealth and prosperity. Too late did she realize it obscured dark circles under their eyes from sleepless nights and drugs and alcohol used to drown out a miserable reality. Their smiles were masks behind which their mutilated and demoralized souls hid. Their show of English had been comprised of but a few memorized phrases, the meanings of which they themselves didn't know. "Grandma" was in fact a shrewd and calculating trafficker. She could smell the pack of one thousand rupee notes that would soon be placed in her hand by the brothel owner in exchange for the goods. A desperate but naïve mother longing to give her daughter a bright future proved no match for "Grandma's" expert manipulation.

Towed gruffly along by the "teachers," Pooja asked for the fiftieth time, "Where are you taking me? Where is Dream Catcher School?"

No one offered an answer.

Having briefly seen the brochure they had given to her mother, Pooja knew Dream Catcher School was a bright white building with red trim and rows of classrooms and a great arched entrance and brightly clad children laughing and studying and eating. But so far, she had not caught a glimpse of Dream Catcher School.

The terrified seven-year-old began to cry. Tugging on the teacher's dress, she sobbed, "Where are we going? Where is the school?"

"Shut up or I'll slap you!" was the only answer she received.

On and on Pooja trudged, traversing crowded city streets with no sign of the white and red school or the arched entrance or the happy children. They turned one corner and then another. The street narrowed, and the crowd thinned. Rounding a sharp bend, they cut through a narrow alley and out onto another street.

But this street wasn't a normal street with people bustling here and there and hawkers shouting their wares and children playing. It was eerily deserted. Hardly a soul could be seen. Pooja's feet tripped on the broken pavement as she gazed up at shabby gray buildings rising on either side. Their walls leaned down on her, menacing, windows like scary monster eyes, black holes from which the glass had long ago been broken. Each entrance was accessed by a piece of broken concrete laid as a bridge across stinking open gutters littered with refuse. Half-starved dogs fought over scraps of *roti*, and pigs rooted among discarded liquor bottles half-sunken in black sludge. The doors of the hovels hung open, their dark interiors concealed by filthy curtains.

Abruptly the troop turned in at one of the doorways and Pooja found herself inside. She was whisked down a hallway and pushed into a windowless room. Its furnishings consisted of a cot with a ratty gray blanket, a nightstand and a bare light bulb overhead emitting a faint glow.

"Where am I?" she cried and whirled to face the "teachers." But the door slammed in her face. Outside the heavy steel bolt slid into place. She was trapped.

Pooja lost track of how long she sobbed there on the cot. She cried until she had no more strength, then lay there limp and gasping.

The door opened. Pooja's heart leaped. Had they remembered her? Had they . . . But then terror replaced the glimmer of hope when a rough man stepped inside. For a moment he reminded her of her deceased father. But he was not her father. He bolted the door, and looked at her with a sickening sneer that made everything in her go limp with horror. Her scream shook the walls, but there was no one to listen. The man slammed a liquor bottle on the nightstand and began to loosen his belt.

Thus began Pooja's nightmare. For one year she endured a hellish existence as a sex slave, tortured, abused and crushed.

One day she could take no more. Her spirit desecrated and will broken, without hope and desperate for a means of escape, she climbed the narrow stairwell to the roof of the four-story building. There the little girl who dreamed of becoming a flight attendant spread her arms like an airplane one last time. Her hair flew in the breeze once again . . . as she plummeted to her death on the street below.

Epilogue

*P*ooja is the missing face in our children's home. Like Neha, this treasure enslaved in darkness would have become a shining star if we could have rescued her before she was trafficked.

Thousands of little girls across north India languish in similar danger, waiting for someone to help them. India has been termed the "poisonous hub" of sex trafficking in Asia.[1] The Ganges River area alone sees over 25,000 children trafficked annually. One researcher dubbed it the "touchstone of our success or failure in completing the task of world evangelization" with Christians numbering less than 2 percent of a burgeoning three hundred million people.

Having poured heart and soul into these regions since I first embarked to India in 1996, TellAsia's children's home,

1. Graham Peebles, "Trafficking of Children and Women in India," Counter Punch.org, September 6, 2013, http://www.counterpunch.org/2013/09/06/children -and-women-for-sale/.

school, churches, anti-trafficking initiatives and educational projects are making an impact.

But there's so much more that could be done. One of TellAsia's primary goals is to put an end to child trafficking in northern India and the Nepal border region. The foundation for this massive vision is in place. Our network of native leaders now extends to virtually every county from Delhi to Kathmandu to Calcutta. These dedicated Indian believers and leaders form the human infrastructure based on which education, schools, anti-trafficking awareness and children's homes can be developed. But scarce funding enables us to conduct these interventions on a relatively limited scale. Hundreds and thousands await our help.

My request as you conclude the reading of this book is threefold:

1. Remember: "Religion that God our Father accepts as pure and faultless is this: to look after orphans and widows in their distress" (James 1:27).

2. Remember the abandoned girls and the Nehas and Poojas of northern India, who face a horrific future of abuse and slavery if not rescued.

3. Help us reach them before the traffickers do.

Here we stand upon the land
    Dungeon keys in nail-scarred hands
On we ride, the King and I,
    Deputies of liberty, raiders of the night.
You warlords of the mount and vale
    Trespassers on this turf,
Your time has come to be undone,
    Captivity's ransom His blood has won.
Give back the ragged treasures,
    broken slaves in darkness bound.
Give back the newborn girls that lie
    abandoned on the ground.
O chains of dearth, disease and death,
    O brothel dungeons dark,
Spirits of deceit and doom,
    Child tormentors, hark!
The rightful King has purchased them.
    They aren't your property.
Release you claws, you chains be torn,
    Literacy taught, oppression shorn.
Trafficker waits by the orphan's gate.
    Another day and it's too late.
Come forth, come forth, O righteous host,
    When will your warriors ride?
How long, how long will you tarry afar,
    While treasures in darkness die?

You can be the difference between a brothel and a bright future. Lift a treasure out of darkness to become a shining star.

Dr. **Leanna Cinquanta** is a pioneer missions strategist, an international motivational speaker and the founder of TellAsia Ministries based in Denver, Colorado. She nurtures and equips native leaders in some of the most difficult areas of the world, annually leading tens of thousands to Christ and providing education to thousands of needy children. Leanna is a graduate of Fuller Theological Seminary and received Regent University's Outstanding Graduate award in completion of her D.Min. degree. Dr. C. Peter Wagner called her "the most competent field missiologist" he has ever known.

At age fifteen Leanna was a self-declared atheist, until she experienced a dramatic face-to-face encounter with Jesus. Her unique, faith-boosting salvation testimony has been featured on TBN, Daystar and many other TV stations. Responding to vivid dreams, in 1996 Leanna forsook a budding equestrian career and set out to bring God's love to a region of the world then known as "the graveyard of Christianity." In the next nineteen years, prayer, persistence and persecution along with miracles of healing and deliverance resulted in the "graveyard" becoming a vineyard with hundreds of thousands finding freedom, salvation and hope.

A visionary who discovers hidden strategies to reveal Christ to today's world, Leanna also has leveraged a little-known method by which she influences millions every year toward Christ with only a few hours of work and zero money. She is a motivational speaker and author of the life transformation series Kingdom Impact. Firmly grounded in Scripture and enlivened with amazing God-stories from twenty years of pioneering the Gospel into tough places, her high-energy messages draw listeners to the edge of their seats. Her ministry is an infusion of radical faith, global vision and out-of-the-box strategy.

Leanna is an instructor in YWAM, the Wagner Leadership Institute and the Perspectives Course. Her passion and joy is to equip others into their adventure of transforming lives with God's love and their destiny of impacting the world as ambassadors of light. She is also committed to cultivating collaboration between Christian groups in order to reveal Christ's love to the world.

One of the visionary initiatives Leanna and her native teams are undertaking is a multidirectional attack on child trafficking and child slavery in north India, with the goal of reducing it by 90 percent. India accounts for 40 percent of the world's slaves and 35 percent of global human trafficking. Leanna and TellAsia seek partners and sponsors to enable this massive vision that will rescue and liberate tens of thousands of needy children into a bright future.

For more information:
Leanna Cinquanta
TellAsia Ministries
12650 W. 64th Ave. #245
Arvada, CO 80004

970-985-8744
888-887-6066

www.tellasia.org
www.leannacinquanta.com

info@tellasia.org
info@leannacinquanta.com